the organic dog biscuit COOKBOOK

from the Bubba Rose BISCUIT COMPANY

by
Jessica Disbrow Talley and Eric Talley

CIDER MILL PRESS

BOOK PUBLISHERS

KENNEBUNKPORT, MAINE

13 Digit ISBN: 978-1-933662-95-4
10 Digit ISBN: 1-933662-95-6

This book may be ordered by mail from the publisher. Please include $2.00 for postage and handling. Please support your local bookseller first!

Books published by Cider Mill Press Book Publishers are available at special discounts for bulk purchases in the United States by corporations, institutions, and other organizations. For more information, please contact the publisher.

Cider Mill Press Book Publishers
"Where good books are ready for press"
12 Port Farm Road
Kennebunkport, Maine 04046
Visit us on the web!
www.cidermillpress.com

Design by Jessica Disbrow Talley
Printed in China

4 5 6 7 8 9 0

acknowledgments

To all the people who made this book possible, we want to say a huge THANK YOU!

To my mom, for all her love, support, infinite help, and hard work. We couldn't have done it without you.

To my dad, for instilling the drive and innate know-how to turn dreams into reality.

And to my brother, Vince, for always being there when we needed you.

A big thank-you to Park Slope, Brooklyn, for generously welcoming us and opening so many doors.

Thank you to Erin McWilliams for all her knowledge and nutritional advice.

Thank you to John Whalen and Dominique De Vito for making this book happen.

And of course to Bob, Rose, and Weeble, our beloved pups; without them we wouldn't have done any of this.

table of contents

About Bubba Rose
Biscuit Company

222

introduction

The Bubba Rose Biscuit Company was founded out of a desire to give dogs healthier treats and food. Tired of looking at long lists of preservatives and poor-quality ingredients in dog treats, and with an awareness about what we eat and where it comes from, we at Bubba Rose Biscuit Company became inspired to create treats from high-quality ingredients from foods we knew more about. We felt our dogs deserved it. Honestly, a bacon treat should actually contain bacon, not a laundry list of chemicals and artificial ingredients, right? We also thought everyone deserved to have their own recipes they could whip up at home for their good pups or on a special occasion – in fact, on any day. Dogs do know the difference with these homemade treats, we're certain of it. So try them out! There are lots of recipes in this book to choose from, and we guarantee your dog will be happy you put forth the effort.

ᘓ It's Organic! ᘔ

With people spending more time and energy to find out where their food comes from and how it is made, it's natural that their focus should turn, too, to wanting to know more about what they feed their pets. My husband Eric and I are both vegetarians, and we are careful about what we eat and where our food comes from, which led us to do the same for our dogs. After thoroughly researching our options, we decided to switch our dogs over to a raw diet made from organic produce and organically raised livestock. There is a lot to learn about this type of diet, but there is no reason your dog's treats can't be as healthy and natural as their food. (For more information on feeding raw, check out the Resources section in the back of the book.)

There are so many organically grown and manufactured products out there to choose from you should have no problem finding the best ingredients to make your treats out of. And if you do run into a problem finding an organic ingredient listed in any of these recipes, you can always swap it out for its non-organic counterpart (try to find a quality alternative, though). Your homemade treats aren't being certified, so do your best to make them with top-notch ingredients and your dogs will love you for it. We promise!

ꙓ Wheat, Corn & Soy Free Ꙕ

Every recipe in this book is free of wheat, corn and soy – the most common sources of food allergies in dogs. Avoiding these ingredients and still producing healthy, tasty treats is not hard – even in over 100 recipes! We know that dogs love treats so much they'll eat them regardless of the fact that their ingredients might make them itchy or not feel well afterwards. Using the recipes in this book, you can take pride in knowing your dogs (and any dog to whom you give these treats) will be happier and healthier for it.

ꙓ The Pantry List Ꙕ

This is a list of the dry ingredients used most frequently in the recipes in this book. Keeping them stocked and handy will make it easy for you to bake a fresh, quality treat for your dog any day of the week.

Organic oat flour
Organic brown rice flour
Organic oat bran
Organic, all-natural peanut butter
    (or peanuts to grind your own; it's easy to do)
Organic honey
Organic applesauce (unsweetened)
Wild caught canned tuna and/or salmon

ε Stock the 'fridge (and freezer too) Ʒ

Besides the ingredients listed above, there are a few items to have on hand in your refrigerator (or to keep frozen in the freezer) so you'll have them whenever you want to make treats.

Organic, shredded cheddar cheese
    (save time and buy pre-shredded)
Organic, grated parmesan cheese
    (save time and buy pre-grated)
Organic eggs
Organic bacon
    (this works especially well if you cook and drain it, then freeze it, so there is always some on hand when the mood strikes to bake dog treats)
Beef or chicken livers
    (these have a very short shelf life in the refrigerator, so buy them when you plan to bake, or freeze immediately for future use)
Organic chicken, turkey or beef
    (next time you are cooking any of these for your dinner, cook some without any seasonings or sauces and freeze it so you'll have the pre-cooked meat ready to use in your baking)

ξ Substitutions ϟ

Baking dog biscuits is not rocket science. Things can easily be exchanged, added, or omitted, depending on what you have available or what your dog particularly likes. These recipes are all very easily adjustable. If you are making substitutions, just keep an eye on the dough consistency when mixing. If it's too dry, add more water. Too wet, add more flour. It's pretty simple. And keep an eye on the baking time. If they are browning faster than the time says, remove them from the oven. If they still look too light, add a few more minutes and keep an eye on them. Your dogs will love most things you make for them, so know they'll be happy even if you think you over- or under-cooked them a bit. Just be sure the meats you add are prepared according to the directions in the recipes.

ξ Tools of the Trade ϟ

The following is a list of utensils and kitchen tools used in many of the recipes in this book; we highly recommend them. If you don't have them, there are alternatives to use, or you can mix and stir by hand. But from experience, we can say that the easier these are to make, the better. The more effort and mess that goes into these treats, the less likely you are going to want to make them again.

Rolling pin

So many of these recipes require you to roll out the dough before cutting it with either a cookie cutter, knife, pizza cutter or upside-down glass. You can cut the dough with many different items, but you really need the rolling pin to flatten the dough. They make nonstick rolling pins, which are a nice investment (you really don't want tuna in your next batch of cookies). But if you don't have one, to prevent the dough from sticking to your rolling pin (which happens since a lot of these doughs are a little sticky to work with) we recommend using a large plastic food-grade storage bag and placing it on top of your lightly floured dough - then roll away. It works like a charm.

Food processor

This truly is your kitchen wonder tool. You can use the grinding attachments to puree liver, make your own peanut butter, chop the cooked vegetables and meats down to fine pieces, etc... Besides, once you've finished the prep work, you switch to your dough attachment and let the machine mix the dough for you. You will still need to scrape the sides, but it cuts down on so much of the work you'll need to do. These machines are great; if you don't have one we wholeheartedly recommend them for your own personal use, as well. In our opinion, every kitchen should have one.

Parchment paper

This makes clean-up a breeze. You don't want liver in the corners of your good cookie or jelly roll pans, do you? If you line your normal baking pans and sheets with a sheet of parchment paper first, all you have to do is peel it off and toss it when you're done, and your pans are ready for the next batch of oatmeal cookies you decide to whip up.

Cutting mat

We love the thin, plastic dishwasher-safe ones. Besides cutting and prepping your food on them, they are flexible, so you can curl them and slide all your ingredients directly into the mixing bowl.

Latex gloves

Some of the ingredients in the treats can be slightly unpleasant to work with. Who wants to mix a dough with tuna or liver in it and risk the smell permeating your hands when you work with it? Throw on a pair of disposable latex gloves (any supermarket carries them in their cleaning aisle) and work away. When you are done, drop them in the trash and keep your hands looking and smelling the way they should.

Cooking pans

This book contains a lot of recipes that use your standard cookie sheet or jelly roll pan. Some flat pan is probably necessary. There are also some recipes that require a muffin pan, mini muffin pan, mini loaf pans and square baking pans. If you don't have any of these, you can always skip that recipe and pick one for which you do have the pans - or substitute with something you have on hand. If you choose an alternate pan, know that you will need to keep an eye on the baking times, as they differ with the different thicknesses of the doughs or mixtures you are using.

ξ Clean-Up Time ʒ

As mentioned previously, covering your pans with parchment paper is a great way to help save time during clean-up (and maintain the sweet integrity of your favorite cookie sheet). Also, using latex gloves will keep the smell off your hands. As stated in the recipes, when you are finished grinding up any of the less-than-pleasant-smelling ingredients – especially liver - rinse out your food processor immediately. These can become caked on very quickly and the dishwasher (or you and a sponge) will have a hard time getting them off. One lesson learned the hard way (we've had it happen, trust us, it's bad) and you'll always rinse those items immediately from now on.

Ɛ Storage Tips Ʒ

Remember these recipes are all for homemade, preservative-free treats. With that in mind, they can't sit out the way processed dog treats that come in cardboard boxes can. We recommend storing any of these fresh-baked goodies in a plastic bag or container in the refrigerator. Even in there they will still mold, like your leftovers, so store only an amount you think you will use within a week. Any extras (since these recipes yield more than a week's worth of treats for most households) can be frozen to thaw out later (this works great) or given away as gifts to your friends, neighbors, or coworkers. Homemade dog biscuits are a great item to share. Spread the happiness!

Ɛ Yields Ʒ

We tried to make these recipes as simple as possible and recommend using whatever you have on hand to form the shapes of the treats. That said, we can not state precisely how many treats each recipe will make. We also don't know your intended audience. If you have a Chihuahua, you'll obviously want to make smaller-sized treats (they'll also cook faster, so keep an eye on them). And if a Great Dane is your canine companion, make them larger (again, watch them, then they might need a little longer to cook). It's up to you, your dogs and what you have on hand. Most of the recipes are about the same size, so once you make one, you'll know how many extras you'll have the next time around.

ε Soft or Crunchy? 3

You know your dogs and their tastes or dietary needs. If you want the treats to be softer, cook them a little less or on a lower heat (definitely keep them in the refrigerator, too). If you want your treats to be a little harder, cook them longer at a lower heat. Or, when they are finished cooking, turn the oven off but leave them in there on the tray to cool for a few hours or overnight. Remember, this is all supposed to be an easy and fun thing to do for your beloved dogs. If they don't turn out perfectly, I bet you they won't mind one bit and will be so happy you made something special for them anyway.

ℰ Chapter 1 ℈

FORGET-me-nots

ℰ **A new and special treat for your favorite four-legger for each month of the year.** ℈

Life without celebrations would be no fun at all, would it? Granted some are more special than others – birthdays, for example, are preferable to Flag Day – but all remind us of something worth taking the time out of our busy lives to observe and appreciate.

Dogs are lucky in that they need nothing more than our very presence to find cause for celebration. Still, occasions marked with particularly yummy treats soon become particularly special for them. When dogs see that turkey being stuffed for Thanksgiving, they know leftovers are imminent. Boxes of chocolates that appear for Valentine's, Easter, and other holidays signal to them that something special is happening (I've included recipes that provide for chocolate substitutes so dogs will no longer be robbed of this delicacy).

When all is said and done, if there's an event worth celebrating with family and friends, there's no reason not to include something special for your four-footed son(s) or daughter(s). Here are 12 recipes to correspond with a significant celebration in every month of the year.

Note: Choose to use organic ingredients in these recipes, as we do when we make them.

❖ it's a ❖
formal affair

Usher in the New Year on the right paw. If you're staying home and enjoying a festive dinner with family and friends, consider going black tie to transform the evening into a memorable, formal affair. Dogs look great with their tuxes and tails on, too, and when they greet your guests at the door looking spiffy with a black bow-tie or tiara on, everyone will know there's a party goin' on. Watch that your guests don't go for these scrumptious-looking black-and-white cookies; they'll be tempted!

FOR THE DOUGH:

1 c. oat flour

1 1/4 c. brown rice flour

1/2 c. peanut butter (unsalted)

1 Tb. honey

1 egg

1/2 c. water

FOR THE TOPPING:

8 oz. carob chips (do not substitute with chocolate)

8 oz. white chocolate chips (these are safe for dogs)

Preheat oven to 350°. Combine all dough ingredients together and mix until a dough forms. Roll out on a lightly floured surface to ¼" thickness. Use a round cookie cutter or the rim of an upside down glass to cut out 2" circles in the dough. Reform and reroll the dough to get as many circles from it as possible.

Place the circles on an ungreased cookie sheet (they can be rather close together as they don't grow much while cooking). Bake 20-25 minutes. Transfer and let cool completely on a wire rack.

When the cookies are cooling, prepare the topping. To do so, heat the white chocolate chips over low heat in a double boiler or in the microwave until melted. Dip half of each cookie into the melted white chocolate and place back on a wire rack to cool. Once all cookies are cooled, at least to the touch, heat the carob chips in a double boiler or in the microwave until melted. Dip the other half of each cookie into the melted carob and place back on a wire rack to cool. Store the cookies in a loosely covered container at room temperature or in an airtight container in the refrigerator.

❦ *February* ❧

whole lotta love

At this time of year when it's appropriate to go over-the-top in displaying your affection, go ahead and really shower it on your dog(s). With these healthy, red-colored, heart-shaped cookies, you can go ahead and spoil him knowing you won't be plying him with a lot of artificial ingredients. Natural food colorings are made from plant and vegetable dyes. While you're at it, try your hand at a poem that expresses your love for your best friend. Remember, "Roses are red, violets are blue"...

1 c. oat flour

1 ¼ c. brown rice flour

½ c. grated parmesan cheese

1 6-oz. can tomato paste

1 egg

½ c. water

Natural red food coloring (optional)

Preheat oven to 350°. Combine all ingredients together and mix until a dough forms. Roll out on a lightly floured surface to $\frac{1}{4}$" thickness. Use a heart-shaped cookie cutter (or a knife) to cut out shapes. Place the cookies on an ungreased cookie sheet (they can be rather close together as they don't grow much while cooking). Bake 20-25 minutes. Transfer and let cool completely on a wire rack. Store the cookies in an airtight container in the refrigerator.

Natural Food Colorings

Beet powder is one of many natural food colorants; it's used in the Whole Lotta Love recipe because it's for Valentine's Day. You can change the color or the dough with these other natural colorants for other occasions. Remember, though, that these fruits and vegetables add flavor, too. Use sparingly to be sure your dog will like it and so you don't overpower the other flavors. Also, never use coffee or any kind of grape juice to add color (or flavor) to a recipe as these ingredients are harmful to dogs.

BLUEISH-PURPLE: blueberries (it is very hard to get a natural blue, but blueberries get closer than the other options)
PURPLE: Blackberries
RED: Paprika, Tomatoes
PINKISH-RED: Beets, Strawberries
GREEN: Spinach
YELLOWISH-ORANGE: Turmeric, Curry powder
ORANGE: Annatto

{ March }

luck of the
irish wolfhound

On St. Patrick's Day – March 17 – everyone is Irish for the day. Your preferred method of celebration may be to have a green beer; we don't recommend that you share that particular tradition with your dog, but you can be assured he'll stay close by your bar stool if you have a plate of these with you. And you know what? They taste pretty good with beer, so you may want to nibble on them, too. Here's an Irish Proverb to keep in mind on this special day:

May you have:

A world of wishes at your command.

God and his angels close to hand.

Friends and family their love impart,

and Irish blessings in your heart!

1 c. oat flour

1 c. brown rice flour

1 1/2 c. tightly packed spinach leaves

1/2 c. grated parmesan cheese

1/2 c. oat bran

1 egg

1/2 c. water

Preheat oven to 350°. Puree the spinach leaves in a food processor until smooth. Combine all ingredients together and mix until a dough forms. Roll out on a lightly floured surface to 1/4" thickness. Use a shamrock-shaped cookie cutter (or a knife) to cut out shapes. Place on an ungreased cookie sheet (they can be rather close together as they don't grow much while cooking). Bake 20-25 minutes. Transfer and let cool completely on a wire rack. Store the cookies in an airtight container in the refrigerator.

sniffin' down the bunny trail

For all you hound people out there, you know the thrill that the mention of the Easter Bunny brings for many of your dogs. Is there anything better than ol' Peter Cottontail's fresh scent in the hedgerow? Well, for those deprived of the Real Thing, these treats will surely come in a close second; in fact, they may even keep your super-sniffer away from the stash of goodies you're trying to hide from you-know-who. While you're making these, remember, spring is just around the corner!

FOR THE CAKE:

2 c. oat flour

3 eggs

1/2 c. honey

2 tsp. baking powder

1/2 tsp. baking soda

1 tsp. cinnamon

2 c. pureed carrots

¼ c. safflower oil

1 tsp. vanilla

FOR THE FROSTING:

1 8-oz. package low-fat cream cheese (at room temperature)

2 Tb. honey

Preheat oven to 350°. Peel and dice the carrots, then puree the carrot pieces in a food processor.

Combine the carrots with all the other ingredients in a large bowl and mix thoroughly. Place cupcake papers in a mini muffin pan (or a regular muffin pan). Spoon mixture evenly into the papers, filling close to the top (the mix will not rise very much).

Bake 10-15 minutes if using the mini muffin pan or 20-25 minutes if using a regular-sized muffin pan. Cupcakes are done when a toothpick inserted in the center comes out clean. Let cool completely on a wire rack.

Combine frosting ingredients together and whip until well mixed and fluffy. Decorate the cupcakes. Store the cupcakes in an airtight container in the refrigerator.

flower power

The days are getting longer and warmer; the flowers are blooming; spring has sprung. Celebrate the joy of a new season with these special cookies, infused with a healthy dose of sun-flowers – how perfect!

1 c. oat flour

1 c. brown rice flour

1 c. hulled sunflower seeds (unsalted)

$^1/_2$ c. oat bran

$^1/_4$ c. honey

3 Tbs. applesauce (unsweetened)

1 egg

$^1/_2$ c. water

Preheat oven to 350°. Combine all ingredients together and mix until a dough forms. Roll out on a lightly floured surface to ¼ " thickness. Use a flower shaped cookie cutter (or a knife) to cut into shapes. Place on an ungreased cookie sheet (they can be rather close together as they don't grow much while cooking).

Bake 20-25 minutes. Let cool completely on a wire rack. Store the cookies in an airtight container in the refrigerator.

ε June ੬

grillin' and chillin'

Get out the barbeque, summertime is here! While you're enjoying classic summer dishes like BBQ chicken, ribs, sausages, and burgers paired with potato salad and other goodies, it just wouldn't be right not to have something equally scrumptious and appropriate for your dog. These cookies are like cheeseburgers with all the fixings – including a dose of healthy sesame seeds and parsley (in fact, you may want to try adding these to your burgers!).

1 c. oat flour

1 c. potato flour

1 c. shredded low-fat cheddar cheese

1 c. lean ground beef (pre-cooked and drained)

1 6-oz. can tomato paste

2 Tb. sesame seeds

1 Tb. dried parsley

1 egg

$\frac{1}{2}$ c. water

Preheat oven to 350°. Cook and drain ground beef. Combine all ingredients (except the sesame seeds) together and mix until a dough forms. Form into hamburger shaped patties (about 2" in diameter). Line a cookie sheet with parchment paper (makes for easy cleanup and keeps ground beef off your cookie sheets). Place on cookie sheet (they can be rather close together as they don't grow much while cooking) and sprinkle the sesame seeds on top.

Bake 20-25 minutes. Transfer and let cool completely on a wire rack. Store the cookies in an airtight container in the refrigerator.

ξ July ϡ

red, white and 'ol blue

It's fun to make a cake that looks like the American flag with strawberries and blueberries on the 4th of July, but these sensational summer fruits can – and should – be enjoyed all month. Their benefits are available for your dog, too, in these fruit-filled, naturally sweetened cookies.

1 ¼ c. oat flour

1 ¼ c. brown rice flour

½ c. oat bran

½ c. strawberries (fresh or frozen)

½ c. blueberries (fresh or frozen)

2 Tbs. honey

1 tsp. cinnamon

1 egg

¼ c. water

Preheat oven to 350°. Puree strawberries and blueberries in a food processor.

Combine all ingredients together and mix until a dough forms. Roll out on a lightly floured surface to ¼" thickness. Use any fun patriotic-shaped cookie cutter (or a knife) to cut into shapes. Place on an ungreased cookie sheet (they can be rather close together as they dont grow much while cooking).

Bake 20-25 minutes. Transfer and let cool completely on a wire rack. Store the cookies in an airtight container in the refrigerator.

❦ August ❧
pawlickin' chicken

Did you know that late July through mid August are considered the "dog days of summer"? The term (*caniculares dies*) was coined by the ancient Romans, who saw Sirius the dog star rising alongside the sun during this time, and who thought that the brightness of the star contributed to the heat of the sun. You can share the phenomenon with your dog with these blazin' BBQ bites (not spicy, just tangy), and possibly do some stargazing, as well!

1 c. oat flour

1 c. brown rice flour

1 c. ground chicken (cooked)

½ c. oat bran

2 Tbs. BBQ Sauce
    (be sure to avoid a sauce that contains onions)

1 egg

½ c. water

Preheat oven to 375°.

Combine all ingredients together and mix until a dough forms. Roll out on a lightly floured surface to ¼" thickness. Use any shaped cookie cutter (or a knife) to cut into shapes. Line a cookie sheet with parchment paper (for easy clean up), and place the cookies on the sheet (they can be rather close together as they don't grow much while cooking).

Bake 22-27 minutes. Transfer and let cool completely on a wire rack. Store the cookies in an airtight container in the refrigerator.

Avoid the Onions

We rely on onions to add flavor to many of our summer favorites, and it's often included in barbeque sauces. They don't harm us (though raw onions make for bad breath), but they have been shown to cause damage to dogs' red blood cells, which can lead to anemia. It's best to avoid all forms of onion in the food you give your dogs – raw, cooked, and even powdered.

₠ September ₡

an apple
a day

Apples are wonderful for everyone, dogs included! There's nothing like a crisp, juicy apple to signal the beginning of fall. You can feed your dog pieces of raw apple as a snack (they love to crunch them just like we do), or cook the apples down into a soft sauce (no sugar!) and add a spoonful or two to their meals. This recipe brings out the great flavor of apples with some cheddar cheese and honey – a recipe no dog can resist!

1 c. oat flour

1 c. brown rice flour

$^1\!/_2$ c. oat bran

1 c. applesauce (unsweetened)

$^1\!/_2$ c. shredded low-fat cheddar cheese

2 Tbs. honey

1 egg

$^1\!/_3$ c. water

Preheat oven to 350°.

Combine all ingredients together and mix until a dough forms. Roll out on a lightly floured surface to ¼" thickness. Use an apple-shaped cookie cutter (or a knife) to cut into shapes. Place on an ungreased cookie sheet (they can be rather close together as they don't grow much while cooking).

Bake 20-25 minutes. Transfer and let cool completely on a wire rack. Store the cookies in an airtight container in the refrigerator.

ξ *October* ξ

bark 'o lanterns

As you're preparing costumes for yourself, your kids, and your dog(s) for the magical day of Halloween, look for recipes that include pumpkin – that super-nutritious vegetable that is the centerpiece of so many Halloween and fall celebrations. For yourself and your family, make a pumpkin soup or pumpkin bread. For your dog, make these Bark 'O Lanterns. With your tummies full, you'll be ready to turn your attention to carving the most glorious pumpkins.

1 c. oat flour

1 c. brown rice flour

1/2 c. pumpkin (canned or fresh)

2 Tbs. molasses (regular or blackstrap)

1 tsp. cinnamon

1 egg

Preheat oven to 350°.

Combine all ingredients together and mix until a dough forms. Roll out on a lightly floured surface to ¼" thickness. Use a pumpkin-shaped cookie cutter (or a knife) to cut into shapes. Then, use a knife to cut out eyes and a mouth (and a nose if you can fit it). Place on an ungreased cookie sheet (they can be rather close together as they don't grow much while cooking).

Bake 20-25 minutes. Transfer and let cool completely on a wire rack. Store the cookies in an airtight container in the refrigerator.

all the trimmings

A favorite "thanks-giving" song goes: "Come ye thankful people come, raise the song of harvest home, all is safely gathered in, 'ere the winter storms begin." At this time of plenty, when preparations are made for the Thanksgiving feast that heralds the holiday season, dogs get excited, too. They see lots of food being made, family and friends getting together, tables being set for a special feast – and they want to share in the good times and good eats. Save the fatty gravy and skins that can lead to digestive upset in dogs for yourself, and make these cookies, which are miny Thanksgiving meals in themselves – irresistible, and healthy.

1 c. ground turkey (cooked)

2 c. brown rice flour

2 eggs

½ c. dried cranberries

½ c. pureed carrots

1 c. cooked, mashed sweet potatoes (or yams)

2 Tbs. honey

1 tsp. dried rosemary

1 tsp. ground cinnamon

Preheat oven to 375°. Peel and dice carrots. Place in a food processor and puree. Cook and mash sweet potatoes.

Combine all ingredients together and mix until a dough forms. Roll out on a lightly floured surface to ¼" thickness. Use any shaped cookie cutter (or a knife) to cut into shapes. Line a cookie sheet with parchment paper. Place on cookie sheet (they can be rather close together as they don't grow much while cooking).

Bake 22-27 minutes. Transfer and let cool completely on a wire rack. Store the cookies in an airtight container in the refrigerator.

ℰ December ℨ

great
dandy canes

For so many, the holiday season comes alive through baking. The kitchen becomes a place to create special cookies, breads, preserves – goodies that make friends and family feel special and welcomed, and that can be wrapped in festive papers to create the perfect gift. Candy canes are a favorite treat this time of year, and dogs can now enjoy them, too – in the form of these fun cookies.

1 $1/2$ c. oat flour

1 $1/2$ c. brown rice flour

$1/2$ c. oat bran

$1/2$ c. grated parmesan cheese

1 6-oz. can tomato paste

$1/2$ tsp. peppermint oil

1 egg

$1/2$ c. water

Natural red food coloring (optional)

Preheat oven to 350°.

Combine flours, oat bran, cheese, egg and water together and mix until a dough forms. Once dough is formed, separate it in half and set one half aside. Return the other half to the mixing bowl, add the peppermint oil and tomato paste, and mix thoroughly, turning it into flavored red dough. Roll out strips of each dough (the red dough and the white dough), about ½" in diameter. Twist them together and cut every 5 inches. Take the twisted 5"-long piece and curl the top down, making it into a candy cane. Continue with the rest of the dough. Place on an ungreased cookie sheet (they can be rather close together as they don't grow much while cooking).

Bake 20-25 minutes. Transfer and let cool completely on a wire rack. Store the cookies in an airtight container in the refrigerator.

Alternate: These can also be turned into wreaths by connecting the two ends, forming a circle.

ξ Chapter 2 ϡ

the sandwich BOARD

☞ The Daily Specials – All the Classics

Don't you love going into one of those classic American diners and finding a sandwich menu that's several pages long and includes some one-of-a-kind concoctions? It makes your mouth water just to consider the possibilities! So imagine how your dog will feel when he gets to sample from this menu. If you have several of these flavor varieties on hand, you can even let him choose his favorite for the day – just as you do at the diner!

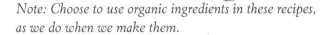

Note: Choose to use organic ingredients in these recipes,
as we do when we make them.

biscuits
and gravy

1 c. oat flour

1 c. brown rice flour

2 tsp. baking powder

$\frac{1}{4}$ c. extra-virgin olive oil

2 ground sweet Italian turkey sausages

$\frac{1}{2}$ c. chicken broth

✳ ✳ ✳

Preheat the oven to 450°. Place the sausages in a pot of water. Bring to a boil and cook for 20 minutes. Remove from heat and run under cold water until cool enough to handle. Remove the sausage casings and finely grind the sausage in a food processor.

Combine the cooked, ground sausage with all ingredients and mix thoroughly until a dough forms. Roll the dough out on a lightly floured surface to $\frac{1}{4}$" thickness. Use a round cookie cutter or the rim of an upside down glass to cut 2"round circles out of the dough. Place on a cookie sheet lined with parchment paper (they can be rather close together as they don't grow much while cooking).

Bake 22-27 minutes or until the tops are golden brown. Remove from oven and let cool completely on a wire rack. Store in an airtight container in the refrigerator.

Broth vs. Gravy

Like the recipes in the cookbooks you use, the ones here feature ingredients that you would normally purchase from a store. One of these is chicken broth (or beef or vegetable broth). If you want to really spoil your dog (and the rest of your family), you can make these broths at home, then refrigerate them so you have them handy to use in your recipes. A broth is essentially the juice that's created when meat or vegetables are steamed or boiled. Don't substitute gravy, which is a broth-based food that's had other things mixed into it to thicken or stabilize it – usually corn starch. Besides that, our recipes are corn-free, as the grain is a potential source of allergies in dogs.

new york–style pretzels

₹ *Street food extraordinaire!* ₹

FOR DOUGH:

1 ½ c. oat flour

1 ½ c. brown rice flour

½ c. oat bran

½ c. grated parmesan cheese

1 egg

⅔ c. chicken broth

FOR TOPPING:

3 Tbs. sesame seeds

1 egg

* * *

Preheat oven to 350°. Combine all dough ingredients and mix thoroughly until a dough forms. Roll out on a lightly floured surface into long strips (about $1/4$" - $1/2$" in diameter). Form into pretzel shapes (adjust the size according to the size of dog you are giving them to). Place the pretzels on an ungreased cookie sheet (they can be close together as they don't spread much while cooking).

Take the remaining egg and beat it in a separate bowl. Use a pastry brush to brush the tops of each pretzel. Sprinkle the sesame seeds over them evenly.

Bake for 25-30 minutes or until golden brown. Remove from the oven and let cool completely on a wire rack. Store in an airtight container in the refrigerator.

just plain cheeseburger

{ It's just a plain old cheeseburger – Oh, so tasty }

1 c. oat flour

1 c. brown rice flour

1 egg

1 c. lean ground beef (pre-cooked and drained)

$\frac{1}{2}$ c. shredded low-fat cheddar cheese

$\frac{1}{4}$ c. tomato paste

$\frac{1}{2}$ c. water

Preheat oven to 350°. Combine all ingredients and mix thoroughly until a dough forms. Dough may be sticky, use flour liberally while rolling. Roll out on a floured surface to $\frac{1}{4}$" thickness. Use a round cookie cutter or the rim of an upside down glass to cut into 2" circles. Place the rounds on a cookie sheet lined with parchment paper (for easy clean up and to keep ground beef off your favorite cookie sheet). They can be rather close together as they don't grow much while cooking.

Bake 20-25 minutes or until tops are golden brown. Remove from the oven and let cool completely on a wire rack. Store in an airtight container in the refrigerator.

☞ Preparing the Beef

We ask that you precook the ground beef in this and other recipes in this book because it results in the safest end-product for your dog. Even if you start with organic, grass-fed beef (or other meat), you want to make sure that any harmful bacteria are cooked out, and that you are draining as much of the fat off the cooked meat as possible before adding it to the other ingredients in these recipes.

turkey & swiss

§ ... Hold the mayo! ₹

1 c. oat flour

1 c. brown rice flour

1 c. grated Swiss cheese

1 c. ground turkey (cooked)

$^1/_2$ c. oat bran

1 Tb. dried parsley

1 egg

$^1/_2$ c. water

Preheat oven to 375°. Combine all ingredients and mix thoroughly until a dough forms. Roll the dough out on a lightly floured surface to $^1/_4$" thickness. Use a cookie cutter or a pizza cutter to cut out shapes. Place on a cookie sheet lined with parchment paper (do you really want turkey on your chocolate chip cookie pans?). They can be close together as they don't spread much while cooking.

Bake for 22-27 minutes or until golden brown. Remove from the oven and let cool completely on a wire rack. Store in an airtight container in the refrigerator.

👉 Substitutions, Just do it!

The great thing about baking your own dog treats is that you can substitute many of the ingredients for items you have on hand or that you know your dog prefers. Since these flours are a little tricky to work with, I would avoid swapping those out as the recipe will require a good amount of adjusting with a different flour. But the main "flavor" ingredients can easily be switched around. For example, the above recipe calls for turkey and Swiss cheese. What if you have roast beef and provolone? Go ahead and use them instead. It's that easy throughout. If you want to swap tuna for salmon or chicken for turkey in a recipe, feel free. *Take note*, however: NEVER substitute an ingredient that may be toxic to dogs, such as onions, chocolate, raisins, macadamia nuts, and grapes.

cheese, please!

ξ Loved by kids and dogs alike ʒ

1 ½ c. oat flour

1 ½ c. brown rice flour

1 c. shredded low-fat cheddar cheese

½ c. grated parmesan cheese

1 egg

½ c. water

Preheat oven to 350°. Combine all ingredients and mix thoroughly until a dough forms. Roll the dough out on a lightly floured surface to $1/4$" thickness. Use a cookie cutter to cut out shapes. Place on an ungreased cookie sheet (they can be close together as they don't spread much while cooking).

Bake for 20-25 minutes or until golden brown. Remove from the oven and let cool completely on a wire rack. Store in an airtight container in the refrigerator.

pup pizza

{ Brooklyn–style: You know, thin }

FOR DOUGH:

1 c. oat flour

1 c. brown rice flour

1 egg

$^1/_4$ c. part skim milk ricotta cheese

$^1/_3$ c. water

FOR TOPPING:

1 6-oz. can tomato paste

1 c. shredded low-fat mozzarella cheese

1 tsp. dried basil

1 tsp. dried oregano

Preheat oven to 375°. Combine all the dough ingredients together and mix thoroughly until a dough forms. Roll the dough out on a lightly floured surface to ¼" thickness. Use a round cookie cutter or the rim of an upside down glass to cut 2" round circles out of the dough. Place them on an ungreased cookie sheet (they can be rather close together as they don't grow much while cooking). Spread the tomato paste evenly on top of all the circles. Sprinkle the mozzarella cheese, basil and oregano on top of each.

Bake 20-25 minutes or until the cheese is lightly browned. Remove from the oven and let cool completely on a wire rack. Store in an airtight container in the refrigerator.

Alternate: For an extra twist, add a few slices of turkey or other low-fat pepperoni or diced grilled chicken on top of the pizzas before baking.

arroz con pollo

ɛ Muy bueno! ȝ

1 ½ c. oat flour

1 ½ c. brown rice flour

1 c. raw ground chicken

1 c. cooked brown rice

1 Tb. dried parsley

1 egg

½ c. water (or chicken broth)

✳ ✳ ✳

Preheat oven to 350°. Combine all ingredients together and mix thoroughly until a dough forms. Roll the dough out on a lightly floured surface to ¼" thickness. Use a cookie cutter and cut out the treats. Place on an ungreased cookie sheet (they can be rather close together as they don't spread while cooking).

Bake 20-25 minutes or until edges are golden brown. Remove from the oven and let cool completely on a wire rack. Store at room temperature in a loosely covered container.

☞ For the Scholarly Dog

Before he just gobbles up these yummy treats, you may want to educate and inspire your dog by telling him what these Spanish words mean in English. It's so simple it only takes a second. Arroz means rice, and pollo means chicken. Arroz con pollo is rice with chicken, or more familiarly, chicken-and-rice. Si, Si!!

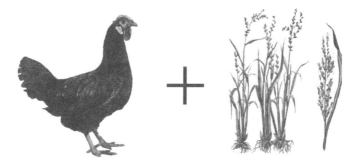

cheese fries

{ The late–night classic. Fortunately, though, these won't keep your dog up all night }

---

1 ½ c. oat flour

1 ½ c. brown rice flour

1 tsp. baking soda

2 tsp. baking powder

]1 c. shredded low-fat cheddar cheese

1 egg

¼ c. extra-virgin olive oil

½ c. water

✳ ✳ ✳

Preheat oven to 450°. Combine all ingredients together (reserving ½ cup cheddar cheese to use later as a topping) and mix thoroughly until a dough forms. Roll the dough out on a lightly floured surface. Separate pieces and form sticks (about 3" long and ½" in diameter). Place on an ungreased cookie sheet (they can be rather close together as they don't grow much while cooking). Sprinkle the remaining cheddar cheese on top of the fries.

Bake 20-25 minutes or until the cheese is lightly brown. Remove from the oven and let cool completely on a wire rack. Store in an airtight container in the refrigerator.

 Oils

There are many kinds of oils available to cook with, and you may be tempted to use something other than extra-virgin olive oil. We list that kind of oil as an ingredient, however, because we feel that it is the kind that is best used by your dog's body. Most vegetable oils are soybean or corn based, and we prefer to use extra-virgin olive oil.

liver & bacon

{ Grandpa's favorite – but hold the onions }

1 ½ c. oat flour

1 ½ c. brown rice flour

½ lb. raw beef or chicken livers

6 slices cooked bacon

1 c. oat bran

1 egg

½ c. water

Preheat oven to 375°. Puree livers in a food processor. Grind bacon into fine pieces in a food processor. Immediately clean the food processor afterwards - you definitely don't want either of these pulverized meats drying in your appliance. Cleaning this up if they do is not easy.

Combine all ingredients and mix thoroughly until a dough forms. Roll the dough out on a lightly floured surface to ¼" thickness. Use any shape cookie cutter or a pizza cutter to slice into individual-sized portions. Place on a cookie sheet lined with parchment paper (keeps the icky ingredients off your cookie sheet and makes clean up a breeze). The treats can be placed close together as they don't spread much while cooking.

Bake for 22-27 minutes or until golden brown. Remove from the oven and let cool completely on a wire rack. Store in an airtight container in the refrigerator.

Note: For crispier treats, do not take them out of the oven to cool. Turn the oven off and let them sit in there overnight. Store in the refrigerator once removed.

☞ Onions – Definitely a No–No

It has recently been reported that onions can be toxic (poisonous) to dogs (and cats). These foods have been shown to cause a form of hemolytic anemia in some animals who ingested them. Hemolytic anemia is a disease of the red blood cells. For this reason, we advice you not to use them in any of our recipes, or in any foods you prepare or give to your dog(s).

west coast especiale

§ *Bite-size burritos – and dogs love 'em!* ₹

1 ½ c. oat flour

1 c. brown rice flour

½ c. oat bran

½ c. lean ground beef (pre-cooked and drained)

¼ c. low-fat sour cream

¼ c. mashed black beans

½ c. shredded jack cheese (or cheddar cheese)

2 eggs

¼ c. water

✳ ✳ ✳

Preheat oven to 350°. Cook the beef and drain thoroughly, then grind in a food processor.

Combine all ingredients and mix thoroughly until a dough forms. Roll out on a lightly floured surface to ¼" thickness. Use an upside down glass to cut into 3 ½" circles. Take each circle and roll it up, making a burrito. Place on a cookie sheet lined with parchment paper (for easy clean up). Treats can be rather close together as they don't grow much while cooking.

Bake 20-25 minutes or until tops are golden brown. Remove from the oven and let cool completely on a wire rack. Store in an airtight container in the refrigerator.

fish & chips

⦃ *The Irish Setter of snack foods* ⦄

1 ¼ c. oat flour

1 c. potato flour

½ c. oat bran

1 c. cooked cod (or another white fish)

1 egg

½ c. water

✳ ✳ ✳

Preheat oven to 350°. Cook the cod thoroughly (use as little oil as possible). Finely grind it in a food processor.

Combine all ingredients and mix thoroughly until a dough forms. Roll the dough out on a lightly floured surface to 1/4"thickness. Use a cookie cutter or a pizza cutter to cut out shapes. Place on a cookie sheet lined with parchment paper (for easy clean up). Treats can be placed close together as they don't spread much while cooking.

Bake for 20-25 minutes or until golden brown. Remove from the oven and let cool completely on a wire rack. Store in an airtight container in the refrigerator.

☞ Fish for Dogs

Everyone knows that fish is good for you, but why? And what about contaminants like mercury or other toxins? To answer the first question, fish is a rich source of important Omega-3 fatty acids. These are the ones that support the optimal functioning of the heart, eyes, immune system, skeletal system, and skin and coat. Supplementing with Omega-3-rich foods can benefit such conditions as allergies, arthritis, heart disease, and even cancer. Of course, it's important to find high-quality sources of fish so that its benefits aren't outweighed by what may be contaminating it – including mercury. That is why we recommend using wild-caught fish in our recipes.

sum-tin

{ ... special in every bite! }

FOR DOUGH:

1 c. oat flour

1 ½ c. brown rice flour

1 tsp. baking powder

1 egg

½ c. chicken broth

FILLING SUGGESTIONS:

Canned pumpkin

Cheese cubes (cheddar's always a favorite)

Small peeled apple pieces

Beef (cooked and ground or in small pieces)

Turkey (cooked and ground or in small pieces)

Bacon (cooked and crumbled)

Tuna

Peanut Butter (unsalted)

Combine all dough ingredients and mix thoroughly until a dough forms. Roll the dough out on a lightly floured surface to ¼" thickness. Use a round cookie cutter or the rim of an upside down glass to cut 2 ½" circles. Place a small amount of any of the suggested fillings - or another of your dog's favorite things - in the center and press the edges up and together making a little bundle. Place on an ungreased cookie sheet (they don't rise, so they can be close together).

Bake for 25-30 minutes or until golden brown. Remove from the oven and let cool completely on a wire rack. Store in an airtight container in the refrigerator.

grilled cheese with bacon

{ A wonderful addition to an all-time favorite }

1 c. oat flour

1 c. brown rice flour

1/2 c. shredded low-fat cheddar cheese

6 slices cooked bacon

1 egg

1/2 c. water

Preheat oven to 350°. Cook bacon slices, then finely grind them in a food processor.

Combine all ingredients and mix thoroughly until a dough forms. Roll the dough out on a lightly floured surface to 1/4" thickness. Use a cookie cutter or a pizza cutter to cut out shapes. Place on a cookie sheet lined with parchment paper (easier clean up). Treats can be placed close together as they don't spread while cooking.

Bake for 20-25 minutes or until golden brown and cheese bubbles up. Remove from the oven and let cool completely on a wire rack. Store in an airtight container in the refrigerator.

meat & potatas

ξ *That's MEAT and POTATAS* 3

1 c. oat flour

1 c. potato flour

½ c. oat bran

1 lb. lean ground beef (pre-cooked and drained)

1 tsp. dried parsley

1 egg

½ c. water

Preheat oven to 375°. Cook and drain ground beef.

Combine all ingredients and mix thoroughly until a dough forms. Roll the dough out on a lightly floured surface to ¼" thickness. Use a cookie cutter or a pizza cutter to cut out shapes. Place on a cookie sheet lined with parchment paper (for easy clean up and to keep beef off your favorite cookie sheet). Treats can be close together as they don't spread while cooking.

Bake for 20-25 minutes or until golden brown. Remove from the oven and let cool completely on a wire rack. Store in an airtight container in the refrigerator.

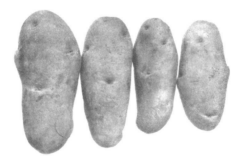

Parsley Packs a Punch

Parsley's role as an attractive garnish has long since been replaced by that of a nutritious and delicious health benefit. Parsley is loaded with vitamins A, B, C, and K and the minerals calcium, potassium, iron, magnesium, phosphorous, as well as protein. It is high in chlorophyll, which gives it the natural freshening power associated with combating foul-smelling breath. All these things make it a great addition to a dog's diet.

liver & cheddar

ξ *Grandma's favorite* Ʒ

1 c. oat flour

1 ½ c. brown rice flour

½ lb. raw chicken liver (or beef liver)

1 c. shredded low-fat cheddar cheese

1 egg

Preheat oven to 350°. Puree the liver in a food processor. Immediately clean the food processor afterwards; once the liver dries it is very hard and unpleasant to get out of there.

Combine all ingredients and mix thoroughly until a dough forms. Roll the dough out on a lightly floured surface to ¼" thickness. Use a cookie cutter or a pizza cutter to cut out shapes. Place on an ungreased cookie sheet (they can be close together as they don't spread much while cooking). Or, for easier clean up, cover the cookie sheet with parchment paper for a no-fuss clean up.

Bake for 20-25 minutes or until golden brown. Remove from the oven and let cool completely on a wire rack. Store in an airtight container in the refrigerator.

✳ ✳ ✳

 # Liver – It's Time to Love It

Liver is an organ meat, and while all carnivores have been feasting on and benefiting from organ meats for as long as they've (we've) been roaming the planet, in the United States today, liver is much maligned as smelly and slimy. Add to that a reputation for being high in cholesterol, and it's no wonder it's not a popular choice for the family dinner table. But liver has long been an acceptable and desired ingredient in dog food and treats – and it's no wonder. Liver is loaded with vitamin A (retinol), which is good for your eyes, skin, and mucous membranes. It also contains vitamins E, D, and K, is packed with essential minerals, is a high-quality protein source, and is rich in omega-3 and omega-6 fatty acids. All these are great for your dog – and for you! One additional note: Because the liver is the detoxifying organ in the body, purchase meat that is as limited in its exposure to toxin-processing as possible, such as an organic cut.

the salty dog

1 ½ c. oat flour

1 ½ c. brown rice flour

¼ c. finely ground pecans

½ c. rolled oats (old-fashioned kind, not instant)

¼ c. blackstrap molasses

1 egg

½ c. water

✳ ✳ ✳

Preheat oven to 350°. Combine all ingredients and mix thoroughly until a dough forms. Roll the dough out on a lightly floured surface to ¼" thickness. Use a cookie cutter or a pizza cutter to cut out shapes. Place on an ungreased cookie sheet (they can be close together as they don't spread much while cooking).

Bake for 20-25 minutes or until golden brown. Remove from the oven and let cool completely on a wire rack. Store in an airtight container in the refrigerator.

☞ Benefits of Molasses

If you're looking for alternative sources of sweeteners in a wide range of foods, one of the ones you should consider is blackstrap molasses. This thick syrup is the by-product of refining sugar: It is the third boiling of the sugar syrup, so it is technically the concentrated byproduct left over after the sugar's sucrose has been crystallized. What's left in this byproduct are lots of beneficial minerals – iron, copper, manganese, magnesium, potassium, and calcium – as well as a dose of vitamin B6. While the taste of blackstrap molasses takes some getting used to (though baked beans or gingersnap cookies wouldn't be the same without it), dogs are typically less discriminating. Ours love the flavor, and we're sure yours will, too.

beef barley

{ The favorite soup du jour turned into a biscuit }

2 c. oat flour

1 ½ c. barley flour

1 c. lean ground beef (pre-cooked and drained)

1 c. pureed carrots

½ c. pureed celery

½ c. oat bran

1 tsp. dried parsley

1 egg

½ c. water

✳ ✳ ✳

Preheat oven to 350°. Cook and drain the ground beef. Peel and dice carrots and celery, then puree in a food processor.

Combine all ingredients and mix thoroughly until a dough forms. Roll the dough out on a lightly floured surface to ¼" thickness. Use a cookie cutter or a pizza cutter to cut out shapes. Place on a cookie sheet lined with parchment paper (for easy clean up). Treats can be placed close together as they don't spread while cooking.

Bake for 20-25 minutes or until golden brown. Remove from the oven and let cool completely on a wire rack. Store in an airtight container in the refrigerator.

☛ Benefits of Barley Flour

Like wheat, barley is a grain that produces seeds that are then ground to produce flour. The benefits of barley compared to wheat include: barley is higher in fiber, contains vitamin E, and has more thiamin, riboflavin, lysine, and essential fatty acids.

liver & oats

ε *Fido's favorite* Ʒ

1 ½ c. oat flour

1 ½ c. brown rice flour

½ lb. raw beef liver (or chicken liver)

1 c. oat bran

1 ½ c. rolled oats (old-fashioned kind, not instant)

1 egg

½ c. water

Preheat oven to 350°. Puree liver in food processor. Immediately clean out food processor afterwards as liver has a tendency to stick, making clean up very unpleasant if left sitting.

Combine all ingredients and mix thoroughly until a dough forms. Roll the dough into 1" diameter ball and place on a cookie sheet covered with parchment paper (to make further clean up just as easy).

Bake for 25 minutes. Turn the oven off and leave treats on the pan in the oven to dry overnight. Store in an airtight container in the refrigerator.

tuna melt

{ Fries not included }

1 c. oat flour

1 c. brown rice flour

$^1/_2$ c. oat bran

1 6-oz. can albacore tuna (in water)

$^1/_2$ c. shredded low-fat cheddar cheese

1 egg

$^1/_2$ c. water

Preheat oven to 350°. Pour entire contents of can of tuna (including all water and juices) into a food processor and finely grind.

Combine all ingredients and mix thoroughly until a dough forms. Add or decrease the water amount a little based on the amount of liquid in the can of tuna. Roll the dough out on a lightly floured surface to $^1/_4$" thickness. Use a cookie cutter or a pizza cutter to cut out shapes. Place on a cookie sheet lined with parchment paper (for easier clean up and to keep tuna off your cookie sheets). Treats can be placed close together as they don't spread while cooking.

Bake for 20-25 minutes or until golden brown. Remove from the oven and let cool completely on a wire rack. Store in an airtight container in the refrigerator.

⧼ Chapter 3 ⧽

the
SILVER
platter

* * * * * * * * * * * * * *

For dogs who live in the lap of luxury

The recipes in Chapter 2 were created for that down-home kind of feeling – comfort food with a kick. These recipes – while equally delicious – are for the more adventurous palette, or to be served to canine friends of your too-classy pooch on special occasions (and let's face it, every day with your dog is a special occasion!). Bon appetit!

Note: Choose to use organic ingredients in these recipes, as we do when we make them.

the opening statement

& Every good meal starts with garlic bread 3

1 ½ c. oat flour

2 c. brown rice flour

1 tsp. baking soda

2 tsp. baking powder

1 tsp. dried rosemary

¼ c. grated parmesan cheese

1 egg

¼ c. olive oil

½ c. water

Preheat oven to 450°. Combine all ingredients together and mix thoroughly until a dough forms. Roll the dough out on a lightly floured surface. Separate pieces and form sticks (about 5" long and 1" in diameter) placing them down on an ungreased cookie sheet (they can be rather close together as they don't grow much while cooking).

Bake 20-25 minutes or until edges are golden brown. Remove from the oven and let cool completely on a wire rack. Store in an airtight container in the refrigerator.

quattro formaggio

§ It's not a party until there's at least four ⅔

1 c. oat flour

1 c. brown rice flour

$\frac{1}{2}$ c. grated parmesan cheese

$\frac{1}{2}$ c. part skim ricotta cheese

$\frac{1}{2}$ c. shredded part skim milk mozzarella

$\frac{1}{2}$ c. grated romano cheese

1 tsp. dried basil

1 tsp. dried oregano

1 egg

$\frac{1}{2}$ c. water

✳ ✳ ✳

Preheat oven to 350°. Combine all ingredients and mix thoroughly until a dough forms. Roll the dough out on a lightly floured surface to $\frac{1}{4}$" thickness. Use a cookie cutter or a pizza cutter to cut out shapes. Place on an ungreased cookie sheet (they can be close together as they don't spread much while cooking).

Bake for 20-25 minutes or until cheese bubbles up and tops are golden brown. Remove from the oven and let cool completely on a wire rack. Store in an airtight container in the refrigerator.

rotisserie chicken

❧ *Old World Flavor – New Dog Taste* ❧

1 c. oat flour

1 c. brown rice flour

½ c. chicken broth

1 c. raw ground chicken

1 Tb. dried rosemary

1 egg

* * *

Preheat oven to 375°. Combine all ingredients and mix thoroughly until a dough forms. Roll the dough out on a lightly floured surface to ¼" thickness. Use a cookie cutter or a pizza cutter to cut out shapes. Place on a cookie sheet lined with parchment paper (for easy clean up). Treats can be placed close together as they don't spread while cooking.

Bake for 22-27 minutes or until golden brown. Remove from the oven and let cool completely on a wire rack. Store in an airtight container in the refrigerator.

 # Lickin' Their Chops for Chicken

Chicken is an ingredient in many dog foods, and for good reason. Besides being a meat that dogs eat readily, it is one of the best meat sources of protein. It also packs a good dose of amino acids, and is easily digestible. Like other meat sources, it's important to select the finest cuts from the best sources to optimize the nutritional benefits.

southwestern sizzler

€ The steak that cooks without fire €

1 ½ c. oat flour

1 ½ c. brown rice flour

1 c. lean ground beef (pre-cooked and drained)

½ c. pureed green peppers

1 Tb. sesame seeds

¼ tsp. cayenne pepper

1 egg

½ c. water

Preheat oven to 350°. Cook and drain the ground beef. Slice the green peppers, discarding the stem, spine and seeds. Puree the pepper slices in a food processor.

Combine all ingredients and mix thoroughly until a dough forms. Roll the dough out on a lightly floured surface to ¼" thickness. Use a cookie cutter or a pizza cutter to cut out shapes. Place on a cookie sheet lined with parchment paper (for easier clean up and to keep ground beef of your cookie sheets). Treats can be placed close together as they don't spread while cooking.

Bake for 22-27 minutes or until golden brown. Remove from the oven and let cool completely on a wire rack. Store in an airtight container in the refrigerator.

Note: Dogs like and can tolerate a little heat - just keep it to a minimum.

gee it's aioli

₹ An Italian staple ₹

1 c. oat flour

1 c. brown rice flour

1 tsp. dried rosemary

1 tsp. dried parsley

1 tsp. dried oregano

½ c. grated parmesan cheese

1 egg

½ c. water

Preheat oven to 350°. Combine all ingredients and mix thoroughly until a dough forms. Roll the dough out on a lightly floured surface to $1/4$" thickness. Use a cookie cutter or a pizza cutter to cut out shapes. Place on an ungreased cookie sheet (they can be close together as they don't spread while cooking).

Bake for 20-25 minutes or until golden brown. Remove from the oven and let cool completely on a wire rack. Store in an airtight container in the refrigerator.

the country club

❧ Tee off on this delicious three-par combination
of apple, cheddar and bacon ❧

1 c. oat flour

1 c. brown rice flour

½ c. shredded low-fat cheddar cheese

½ c. applesause (unsweetened)

½ c. rolled oats (old-fashioned kind, not instant)

6 slices cooked bacon

1 egg

⅓ c. water

Preheat oven to 350°. Cook bacon then finely grind in a food processor.

Combine all ingredients and mix thoroughly until a dough forms. Roll the dough out on a lightly floured surface to ¼" thickness. Use a cookie cutter or a pizza cutter to cut out shapes. Place on a cookie sheet lined with parchment paper (for easier clean up). Treats can be placed close together as they don't spread while cooking.

Bake for 20-25 minutes or until golden brown. Remove from the oven and let cool completely on a wire rack. Store in an airtight container in the refrigerator.

mambo italiano

{ Of course it's got rosemary! }

1 ½ c. oat flour

1 ½ c. brown rice flour

1 6-oz. can tomato paste

½ c. fresh mozzarella, finely chopped

½ c. pureed roasted red peppers (optional)

½ c. grated parmesan cheese

1 tsp. dried rosemary

1 tsp. dried oregano

1 tsp. dried basil

1 egg

½ c. water

Preheat oven to 350°. If using roasted red peppers, puree these in a food processor before doing anything else.

Combine all ingredients and mix thoroughly until a dough forms. Roll the dough out on a lightly floured surface to ¼"thickness. Use a cookie cutter or a pizza cutter to cut out shapes. Place on an ungreased cookie sheet (they can be close together as they don't spread while cooking).

Bake for 20-25 minutes or until golden brown. Remove from the oven and let cool completely on a wire rack. Store in an airtight container in the refrigerator.

 Rosemary for More Than Seasoning

Rosemary – like sage and thyme – is traditionally used to season foods, particularly roasted meats and vegetables. It is becoming more and more appreciated for its medicinal as well as gustatory benefits. Rosemary is a natural antibiotic and antiseptic. It also increases blood flow to the brain, aiding in memory and, when inhaled, rejuvenating the senses. It is a potent herb, and a little goes a long way – we could all use a little more often, though.

walnut-crusted salmon

{ *It's so wild it jumps out of your dish* }

1 ½ c. oat flour

1 ½ c. brown rice flour

1 6-oz. can wild salmon

1 ½ c. finely chopped walnuts

1 Tb. honey

1 Tb. sesame seeds

1 egg

½ c. water

✳ ✳ ✳

Preheat oven to 350°. Empty entire contents of salmon can (including liquid and juices) into a food processor and puree it.

Combine all ingredients (except the walnuts) and mix thoroughly until a dough forms. Roll into 1" diameter balls. Roll the dough balls in the remaining walnuts and squeeze gently in the palm of your hand to press the walnuts into the dough. Place on a cookie sheet lined with parchment paper (for easier clean up). Treats can be placed close together as they don't spread while cooking.

Bake for 22-27 minutes or until tops are golden brown. Remove from the oven and let cool completely on a wire rack. Store in an airtight container in the refrigerator.

☞ Nuts – The Good, the Bad and the Ugly

Many of the recipes in this book contain peanuts, because what dog doesn't love peanut butter? Ok, we've heard of a few, but they are definitely in the minority. Other nuts that are good for dogs (and people) include walnuts, cashews, and almonds. Nuts are an excellent source of protein. But keep in mind that they are also high in fat. One nut to never feed your dog is the macadamia nut. While the exact source of its toxicity is still not known, it is associated with producing muscle tremors and partial paralysis in dogs. If you're going to get nutty, go for the good ones.

cabin by the lake

*§ A natural blend with flaxseed
to enhance your dog's natural beauty 3*

1 c. oat flour

1 c. brown rice flour

½ c. flaxseed meal (or flaxseeds)

½ c. shredded low-fat cheddar cheese

3 Tbs. sesame seeds

1 egg

½ c. water

Preheat oven to 350°. Combine all ingredients and mix thoroughly until a dough forms. Roll the dough out on a lightly floured surface to ¼" thickness. Use a cookie cutter or a pizza cutter to cut out shapes. Place on an ungreased cookie sheet (they can be close together as they don't spread while cooking).

Bake for 20-25 minutes or until golden brown. Remove from the oven and let cool completely on a wire rack. Store in an airtight container in the refrigerator.

☞ Flaxseeds

The seeds of the flax plant have been cultivated for human consumption for millennia. Flaxseed contains lignans, which are particularly beneficial to the female reproductive system. The fiber in flaxseed acts as a natural laxative to aid in digestion; in the intestine, it helps coat the lining, reducing the incidence of constipation, gastritis, and colon conditions. Using ground flaxseed in recipes certainly adds beneficial fiber and digestive support.

the nova scotia special

1 c. oat flour

1 c. brown rice flour

8 oz. lox

8 oz. low-fat cream cheese (at room temperature)

$\frac{1}{2}$ c. oat bran

1 egg

$\frac{1}{2}$ c. water

Preheat oven to 350°. Slice lox and finely grind it in a food processor.

Combine all ingredients and mix thoroughly until a dough forms. Roll the dough out on a lightly floured surface to $^1\!/_4$" thickness. Use a cookie cutter or a pizza cutter to cut out shapes. Place on a cookie sheet lined with parchment paper (for easier clean up and to keep lox off your cookie sheets). Treats can be placed close together as they don't spread much cooking.

Bake for 20-25 minutes or until golden brown. Remove from the oven and let cool completely on a wire rack. Store in an airtight container in the refrigerator.

canine quiche

{ Meaty morsels made especially for your pup }

1 c. oat flour

½ c. oat bran

2 eggs

1 c. lean ground beef (pre-cooked and drained)

1 c. tightly packed spinach leaves

1 c. pureed carrots

✻ ✻ ✻

Preheat oven to 400°. Peel, dice and puree carrots in a food processor. Puree spinach leaves in a food processor until smooth.

Combine all ingredients together and mix thoroughly. Place cupcake papers into a mini muffin pan (or a regular muffin pan). Push mixture evenly into the papers (the consistency will be similar to meatloaf) coming close to the top (the mix will not rise very much).

Bake 10-15 minutes if using the mini muffin pan or 20-25 minutes if using a regular sized muffin pan. Cupcakes are done when a toothpick inserted into the center comes out clean. Remove from the oven and let cool completely on a wire rack. Store in an airtight container in the refrigerator.

Note: A dollop of non-fat cream cheese or sour cream on top of these makes them an extra-special treat.

 Spinach – Lean & Green

There must be something in spinach that enables Popeye to "fight to the finish" after he eats it. What there is is a solid helping of fiber, the minerals calcium and potassium, and the vitamins A, B6, and K. Spinach also has twice the iron content of most other greens, and it is a recognized source of antioxidants. Avoid Popeye's source – canned spinach – and instead choose organically grown regular or baby spinach and feed it lightly steamed or raw (chopped up fine).

asnackadopoulis

ξ *Toto, we're not in Athens anymore* ζ

1 c. oat flour

1 c. brown rice flour

1 c. spinach leaves (pre-cooked and drained)

$\frac{1}{2}$ c. oat bran

$\frac{1}{2}$ c. feta cheese

1 egg

$\frac{1}{2}$ c. water

Preheat oven to 375°. Puree spinach in a food processor.

Combine all ingredients and mix thoroughly until a dough forms. Roll the dough out on a lightly floured surface to $\frac{1}{4}$" thickness. Use a cookie cutter or a pizza cutter to cut out shapes. Place on a cookie sheet lined with parchment paper (for easier clean up). Treats can be placed close together as they don't spread much cooking.

Bake for 22-27 minutes or until golden brown. Remove from the oven and let cool completely on a wire rack. Store in an airtight container in the refrigerator.

the only true pâté

ℰ Why, it's liver of course ℨ

2 c. oat flour

½ c. oat bran

1 lb. raw chicken (or beef) livers

2 eggs

Preheat oven to 375°. Puree the liver in a food processor. Immediately clean out the food processor afterwards. Liver is very hard to get out once it dries, trust us.

Combine all ingredients together and mix thoroughly. Line a 9" square pan with parchment paper (you'll thank us for this) and pour the mixture in.

Bake 35-40 minutes or until sides of seem to be loosening from the pan. Cool completely in the pan. Slice into individual sized pieces. Store in an airtight container in the refrigerator.

a thanksgiving prelude

ξ *An early start for the big day* ʒ

1 ½ c. oat flour

1 ½ c. brown rice flour

1 c. oat bran

1 c. mashed, cooked sweet potato

1 c. raw ground turkey

1 egg

½ c. water

Preheat oven to 350°. Cook and mash the sweet potato.

Combine all ingredients and mix thoroughly until a dough forms. Roll the dough into 1" balls and place on a cookie sheet lined with parchment paper (for easier clean up). Treats can be placed close together as they don't spread while cooking.

Bake for 22-27 minutes or until golden brown. Remove from the oven and let cool completely on a wire rack. Store in an airtight container in the refrigerator.

thatsa one spicy meatball

{ All it needs is a little marinara }

2 lbs. raw, lean ground beef (or turkey)

$^1/_2$ c. grated parmesan cheese

$^1/_2$ c. oat bran

1 tsp. dried oregano

1 tsp. dried parsley

1 egg

* * *

Preheat oven to 350°. Combine all ingredients together and mix thoroughly. Roll mixture into 1" balls and place on a cookie sheet lined with parchment paper (makes for easier clean up). We recommend using rubber or latex gloves to form and roll the meatballs. It's a lot more pleasant that way.

Bake 15-20 minutes or until evenly browned and cooked through. Remove from the oven and let cool. Store in an airtight container in the refrigerator.

Notes: These freeze very well. We recommend placing a small amount in the refrigerator and the rest in a bag in the freezer. When you need more you have them ready and on hand.

take-out royalty

*❧ The most prolific combination
ever to be printed on a Chinese menu ❧*

1 c. oat flour

1 c. brown rice flour

½ c. oat bran

1 c. ground chicken (cooked)

1 c. pureed broccoli

2 Tbs. blackstrap molasses

1 egg

½ c. water

Preheat oven to 350°. Place broccoli in a food processor and puree it.

Combine all ingredients and mix thoroughly until a dough forms. Roll the dough into 1" balls. Place on a cookie sheet lined with parchment paper (makes for easier clean up). Treats can be placed close together as they don't spread much cooking.

Bake for 22-27 minutes or until golden brown. Remove from the oven and let cool completely on a wire rack. Store in an airtight container in the refrigerator.

☞ Broccoli –
It's Hard to Beat

If you're looking for a veggie that packs a wallop of cancer-fighting phytochemicals as well as a solid dose of vitamin C, beta carotene, folic acid, and calcium, then look no farther than the fresh, organic broccoli at your grocery store or farmer's market. Chop or puree it raw before adding it to your dog's meals (or treats), or lightly steam it and cut it up – using the broth created by the steam, too. Good stuff!

ℰ Chapter 4 ℨ

THE cookie ✳ JAR ✳

A little something for the sweet tooth

We all indulge ourselves with sweets, so why not our dogs? They appreciate them, too. As you'll learn from these recipes and the sidebars in this chapter, the key is to give them sweets that won't upset their digestive system and that aren't harmful (remember, never give chocolate to dogs!) With this wide selection of recipes to choose from, you have lots of options to charm your companion through his sweet tooth.

Note: Choose to use organic ingredients in these recipes, as we do when we make them.

the classic

*{ The keystone to any cookie jar —
the doggie version of the chocolate chip cookie }*

1 ¹/₂ c. oat flour

1 ¹/₂ c. brown rice flour

1 c. carob chips (can NOT be substituted with chocolate)

1 egg

1 tsp. vanilla

¹/₂ c. water

Preheat oven to 350°. Combine all ingredients together and mix thoroughly. Roll into small balls (about 1" in diameter) and place on an ungreased cookie sheet (they can be rather close together as they don't spread while cooking). Press each one down with your hand to flatten the cookies.

Bake 18-22 minutes or until edges are golden brown. Let cool completely on a wire rack. Store at room temperature in a loosely covered container.

☞ Carob

Carob pods come from carob trees, which are small evergreen shrubs native to the Mediterranean. Before the use of sugar cane, carob was used as a natural sweetener. In fact, the pods have a taste reminiscent of sweetened cocoa, but without the theobromine, caffeine, or other psychoactive properties of cocoa (which are potentially lethal in dogs). Mixed with saturated fats, carob bars and chips can be safely substituted for chocolate. It is important to remember never to give a dog chocolate.

snickerdoodle-poodle-poos

{ What's in that again? }

1 ½ c. oat flour

1 ½ c. brown rice flour

2 tsp. cinnamon

1 egg

¼ c. honey

1 tsp. vanilla

½ c. water

* * *

Preheat oven to 375°. Combine all ingredients together and mix thoroughly in a large bowl. Spoon out mixture and roll into balls (about 1" in diameter). Place on an ungreased cookie sheet (they can be rather close together as they don't spread while cooking). Using a fork, press down the balls, flattening them and adding decorative lines in the tops.

Bake 18-22 minutes or until golden brown. Let cool completely on a wire rack. Store at room temperature in a loosely covered container.

lumberjack snacks

❧ A cool peanut butter and fruit snack for those hard-working dogs ☙

1 c. rolled oats (the old-fashioned kind, not instant)

1 c. oat bran

$1/4$ c. dried cranberries

$1/4$ c. finely chopped peanuts

$1/4$ c. honey

$1/2$ c. peanut butter (unsalted)

Mix all ingredients together. Drop mixture by tablespoon into mini cupcake papers and place on a rimmed baking sheet or large plate. Put in the refrigerator for 15 minutes, or until set. Store in an airtight container in the refrigerator.

plumpkins

Pumpkin cookies dropped from heaven

1 ½ c. oat flour

1 ½ c. brown rice flour

½ tsp. cinnamon

½ tsp. ground nutmeg

½ tsp. ground ginger

1 egg

3 Tb. applesauce (unsweetened)

¾ c. canned pumpkin (or fresh, pureed pumpkin)

½ c. water

Preheat oven to 350°. Combine all ingredients together and mix thoroughly. Spoon mixture out with a tablespoon and drop onto an ungreased cookie sheet. These cookies will not rise or flatten, so if you want a flatter cookie, press it down before baking.

Bake 18-22 minutes or until golden brown. Let cool completely on a wire rack. Store in an airtight container in the refrigerator.

☞ Out of the Patch, and Into the Bowl

Pumpkin is a nutritious and delicious food whose benefits can be reaped by including it in recipes that go well beyond the traditional holiday pie – and your dog shouldn't be getting any of that pie, anyway! Pumpkin is high in potassium and beta carotene (a natural antioxidant) but low in calories, so when steamed and eaten in chunks or pureed, pumpkin is great for those watching their weight who want to enjoy a flavorful and filling veggie. A tablespoon or two of canned (or fresh) pumpkin added to their food will firm up your dog's stool if he has diarrhea, or help loosen it if he is constipated (it's true, it works both ways). It's a miracle food!

ginger snaps

ℰ *The ginger snaps so you don't have to* ℥

2 c. oat flour

2 c. brown rice flour

2 tsp. baking soda

2 tsp. ground ginger

1 tsp. cinnamon

1 tsp. ground cloves

1 egg

$\frac{1}{4}$ c. safflower oil

$\frac{1}{2}$ c. molasses (blackstrap or regular)

$\frac{1}{2}$ c. water

Preheat oven to 350°. Combine all ingredients together and mix thoroughly. Spoon mixture out with a tablespoon and drop onto an ungreased cookie. These cookies will not rise or flatten, so if you want a flatter cookie, press it down before baking.

Bake 18-22 minutes or until edges are golden brown. Let cool completely on a wire rack. Store at room temperature in a loosely covered container.

☞ Ginger

Besides having a smell that instantly transforms a house into a home (just as a dog does), ginger is a tasty and nutritious spice. It is especially beneficial for stomach upset.

oatmeal cookies

‹ *As good as you remember* ›

1 ½ c. oat flour

1 ½ c. brown rice flour

1 tsp. baking powder

½ tsp. baking soda

2 c. rolled oats (old-fashioned kind, not instant)

1 c. finely chopped peanuts (unsalted)

2 eggs

¼ c. safflower oil

¾ c. peanut butter (unsalted)

½ c. honey

1 tsp. vanilla

✻ ✻ ✻

Preheat oven to 350°. Combine all ingredients together and mix thoroughly. Roll into small balls (about 1" in diameter) and place on an ungreased cookie sheet (they can be rather close together as they don't spread while cooking). Press each one down with your hand to flatten the cookies.

Bake 18-22 minutes or until edges are golden brown. Let cool completely on a wire rack. Store at room temperature in a loosely covered container.

bahama mamas

{ The fruit of the islands }

1 c. oat flour

1 c. brown rice flour

1 c. shredded coconut (unsweetened)

1 egg

$1/2$ c. peanut butter (unsalted)

1 tsp. vanilla

$1/2$ c. water

Preheat oven to 350°. Combine all ingredients together and mix thoroughly. Roll into small balls (about 1" in diameter) and place on an ungreased cookie sheet (they can be rather close together as they don't spread while cooking). Press each one down with your hand to flatten the cookies.

Bake 18-22 minutes or until edges are golden brown. Let cool completely on a wire rack. Store at room temperature in a loosely covered container.

honey mutts

*❦ A sweet honey and oat confection
your pup is sure to love ϡ*

1 ½ c. brown rice flour

2 c. rolled oats (old-fashioned kind, not instant)

1 egg

1 c. peanut butter (unsalted)

4 Tbs. applesauce (unsweetened)

¼ c. honey

¼ c. water

Preheat oven to 350°. Combine all ingredients together and mix thoroughly. Roll into small balls (about 1" in diameter) and place on an ungreased cookie sheet (they can be rather close together as they don't spread while cooking). Press each one down with your hand to flatten the cookies.

Bake 18-22 minutes or until golden brown. Let cool completely on a wire rack. Store in an airtight container in the refrigerator.

energy barks

Powers your dog up for a whole day of digging ⅊

1 ¼ c. oat flour

1 ¼ c. brown rice flour

½ c. rolled oats (old-fashioned kind, not instant)

½ c. granola (can not contain raisins)

1 egg

¼ c. molasses (blackstrap or regular)

½ c. water

Preheat oven to 350°. Combine all ingredients together and mix thoroughly. Roll into small balls (about 1" in diameter) and place on an ungreased cookie sheet (they can be rather close together as they don't spread while cooking). Press each one down with your hand to flatten the cookies.

Bake 18-22 minutes or until edges are golden brown. Let cool completely on a wire rack. Store at room temperature in a loosely covered container.

☞ Rid Your Dog's Pantry of Raisins

Though scientists haven't pinpointed what it is in raisins, especially, that's toxic to dogs, they've seen plenty of cases of acute renal failure in dogs that have eaten various amounts of raisins (and grapes) to know that they contain something quite harmful. Harmful enough that the veterinary community is clear about the fact that raisins and grapes should not be fed to dogs.

cranberry &
white chocolate
chunk cookies

*ε Didn't you say chocolate was bad?
Not white chocolate! ʒ*

1 ½ c. oat flour

1 ½ c. brown rice flour

½ c. dried cranberries

½ c. white chocolate chips or chunks

1 egg

½ c. water

✳ ✳ ✳

Preheat oven to 350°. Combine all ingredients together and mix thoroughly. Roll into small balls (about 1" in diameter) and place on an ungreased cookie sheet (they can be rather close together as they don't spread while cooking). Press each one down with your hand to flatten the cookies.

Bake 18-22 minutes or until edges are golden brown. Let cool completely on a wire rack. Store at room temperature in a loosely covered container.

☞ White Chocolate in Moderation

Why is white chocolate ok for dogs but milk or dark chocolate is an absolute no-no? Because white chocolate is really not chocolate at all. It is a mixture of cocoa butter, sugar, and milk. Originally made in Switzerland, it didn't become popular in the US until the 1980s. Now it is marketed alongside regular chocolates as an equally creamy and sweet confection – and in limited quantities, is a safe addition to canine cookies.

lil' taste o' pie

{ Apple pie – a perennial holiday favorite,
now bite-size for your pup }

1 ½ c. oat flour

1 ½ c. brown rice flour

2 ½ tsp. cinnamon

½ c. oat bran

1 egg

½ c. applesauce (unsweetened)

2 Tbs. honey

½ c. water

Preheat oven to 350°. Combine all ingredients together and mix thoroughly. Roll into small balls (about 1" in diameter) and place on an ungreased cookie sheet (they can be rather close together as they don't spread while cooking). Press each one down with your hand to flatten the cookies.

Bake 18-22 minutes or until edges are golden brown. Let cool completely on a wire rack. Store at room temperature in a loosely covered container.

☞ An Apple a Day

You know the old saying, "An apple a day keeps the doctor away"? The same, thankfully, can be said for dogs. Apples that have been thoroughly washed, then had the stems and seeds removed and are cut up into slices or chunks, make great healthy snacks for dogs. Apples have numerous health benefits.

puppy dog eyes

ℰ Nobody can resist these adorable carob puppy dog eyes! ℨ

1 ½ c. oat flour

1 ½ c. brown rice flour

1 c. carob chips (can not be substituted with chocolate)

1 egg

½ c. peanut butter (unsalted)

½ c. water

Preheat to 350°. Combine flours, egg, peanut butter and water and mix thoroughly. Roll into small balls (about 1" in diameter) and place on an ungreased cookie sheet (they can be rather close together as they don't spread while cooking). Use your thumb to press an indent into the center of each cookie. Evenly sprinkle a few of the remaining carob chips into the center of each cookie (they should pool while cooking and look like a brown dot when cooled).

Bake 18-22 minutes or until edges are golden brown. Let cool completely on a wire rack. Store at room temperature in a loosely covered container.

banana b'oats

₹ Boatloads of oats and bananas ₹

1 ½ c. oat flour

1 ½ c. brown rice flour

1 tsp. cinnamon

1 c. rolled oats (old-fashioned kind, not instant)

½ c. oat bran

1 egg

1/2 c. bananas (mashed & pureed)

½ c. water

Preheat to 350°. Combine all ingredients together and mix thoroughly. Roll into small balls (about 1" in diameter) and place on an ungreased cookie sheet (they can be rather close together as they don't spread while cooking). Press each one down with your hand to flatten the cookies.

Bake 18-22 minutes or until edges are golden brown. Let cool completely on a wire rack. Store at room temperature in a loosely covered container.

pine cones

1 ½ c. oat flour

1 ½ c. brown rice flour

½ c. finely chopped peanuts (unsalted)

¼ c. sesame seeds

½ c. rolled oats (old-fashioned kind, not instant)

2 eggs

¼ c. molasses (blackstrap or regular)

½ c. peanut butter

½ c. water

Preheat oven to 350°. Combine flours, peanuts, oats, egg and molasses together and mix thoroughly. Roll into small balls (about 1" in diameter). Roll the cookie in the sesame seeds and press gently around them to adhere the seeds to the dough. Place on an ungreased cookie sheet (they can be rather close as they don't spread while cooking).

Bake 18-22 minutes or until edges are golden brown. Let cool completely on a wire rack. Store at room temperature in a loosely covered container.

☞ Oats & Oat Bran

Oats are a grain with a low gluten content. They have been shown to lower cholesterol and reduce the risk of heart disease. Oat bran – the hull part of the grain – was so widely thought of as a nutritional supplement that there was an oat bran craze in the early 1990s where everything from muffins to potato chips included it. The craze has passed, but the nutritive values live on. The low glycemic content of oats means they're digested more slowly, sustaining energy for longer.

muddy paws

ℰ *The only acceptable kind to have in the house* Ʒ

1 ½ c. oat flour

1 ½ c. brown rice flour

¼ c. carob powder (can not be substituted with chocolate)

½ c. carob chips (can not be substituted with chocolate)

1 egg

½ c. peanut butter (unsalted)

1 Tb. honey

⅔ c. water

Preheat oven to 350°. Combine all ingredients together and mix thoroughly. Roll into small balls (about 1" in diameter) and place on an ungreased cookie sheet (they can be rather close together as they don't spread while cooking). Press each one down with your hand to flatten the cookies.

Bake 18-22 minutes or until edges are golden brown. Let cool completely on a wire rack. Store at room temperature in a loosely covered container.

☞ Peanut Butter

As oily as it looks, peanut butter is high in monounsaturated fats – the kind that protect against heart disease. Grinding your own (organic) nuts yields a butter of exceptional flavor and avoids the sugars and salts that are often added to commercial varieties. Peanuts are an excellent source of protein, as well.

coconut cremés

*{ It's just like the pie,
but with the convenience of a cookie }*

1 ½ c. oat flour

1 ½ c. brown rice flour

1 c. shredded coconut (unsweetened)

1 tsp. cinnamon

1 egg

½ c. skim milk (or coconut milk)

1 tsp. vanilla

Preheat oven to 350. Combine all ingredients together and mix thoroughly. Roll into small balls (about 1" in diameter) and place on an ungreased cookie sheet (they can be rather close together as they don't spread while cooking). Press each one down with your hand to flatten the cookies.

Bake 18-22 minutes or until edges are golden brown. Let cool completely on a wire rack. Store in an airtight container in the refrigerator.

going nuts

ɛ Your dog's going to go nuts over these crunchers ȝ

1 ½ c. oat flour

1 ½ c. brown rice flour

½ c. finely ground peanuts (or walnuts)

¼ c. sesame seeds

1 c. shelled walnuts (halved)

½ c. oat bran

1 egg

½ c. molasses (blackstap or regular)

1 tsp. vanilla

⅔ c. water

Preheat oven to 350°. Combine all ingredients (except the shelled walnut halves) and mix thoroughly until a dough forms. Roll into small balls (about 1" in diameter) and place on an ungreased cookie sheet (they can be rather close together as they don't spread while cooking). Press one of the walnut halves into the top of each cookie.

Bake 20-22 minutes or until tops are golden brown. Let cool completely on a wire rack. Store in a loosely covered container at room temperature.

red hot
puppermints

*{ These are sure to straighten their tail –
and freshen their breath }*

1 c. oat flour

1 c. brown rice flour

½ c. grated parmesan cheese

¼ tsp. peppermint oil

1 egg

½ c. water

Natural red food coloring (optional)

Preheat oven to 350°. Combine all ingredients together and mix thoroughly. Roll into small balls (about 1" in diameter) and place on an ungreased cookie sheet (they can be rather close together as they don't spread while cooking.

Bake 18-22 minutes or until edges are golden brown. Let cool completely on a wire rack. Store in an airtight container in the refrigerator.

☞ Peppermint

Mints have long been associated with aiding in digestive upset, and this is true for dogs as well as people. They have the added benefit of being able to freshen breath. A double-whammy for dogs!

gingerbread mailmen

{ It's your dog's turn to deliver }

1 ½ c. oat flour

1 ½ c. brown rice flour

1 tsp. baking powder

1 tsp. ground ginger

1 tsp. cinnamon

½ tsp. baking soda

1 egg

¼ c. safflower oil

½ c. molasses (blackstrap or regular)

¼ c. peanut butter (unsalted)

1 Tb. apple cider vinegar

Preheat oven to 350°. Combine all ingredients together and mix thoroughly until a dough forms. Roll the dough out on a lightly floured surface to ¼" thickness. Use a gingerbread man (or any shaped cookie cutter, mail men ones are cute!) cookie cutter and cut out the treats. Place on an ungreased cookie sheet (they can be rather close together as they don't spread while cooking).

Bake 18-22 minutes or until edges are golden brown. Let cool completely on a wire rack. Store at room temperature in a loosely covered container.

 Apple Cider Vinegar

It seems you can't go wrong giving your dog apple cider vinegar – inside and out! The easiest way to introduce it to your dog's regular diet is to put a tiny amount in the water bowl. As he becomes used to the taste, increase the amount ever so gradually until you are adding about a teaspoon a day in the water. ACV is good for arthritis, allergies, itchy skin, correcting pH levels, eliminating tear stains around the eyes, fighting fleas and other pests, and so much more!

neapolitan must-haves

{ Little coloful cookies for big appetites }

FOR DOUGH:

1 $1/2$ c. oat flour

1 $1/2$ c. brown rice flour

$1/2$ c. oat bran

1 tsp. cinnamon

1 egg

$1/4$ c. honey

$1/2$ c. peanut butter (unsalted)

1 tsp. vanilla

$2/3$ c. water

FOR COATING:

$1/2$ c. sesame seeds

Natural green food coloring

Natural red food coloring

$1/2$ c. water

1 egg

Preheat oven to 350°. Take 2 small bowls and fill each with ¼ cup water. Mix the greed food coloring into one dish of water. Then mix the red food coloring in the other bowl of water. Place ¼ cup sesame seeds into each bowl. Stir until all are evenly coated with the colored liquid. Let sit.

Combine all dough ingredients together and mix thoroughly. Drain the remaining liquid from the sesame seeds and place the seeds (keeping the colors separated) onto pieces of parchment paper. Place the parchment with the seeds on it on a cookie sheet and place into the oven for 15 minutes.

While the seeds are drying in the oven, roll the dough into small balls (about 1" in diameter). Take the remaining egg and beat it in a separate bowl. Remove the seeds from the oven, but keep them on the parchment paper.

Dip the top half of each cookie into the egg mixture, then dip it directly into one of the two piles of colored seeds. Place on an ungreased cookie sheet (they can be rather close together as they don't spread while cooking). Repeat this process, alternating colors, for each of the remaining cookies.

Bake 18-22 minutes or until edges are golden brown. Let cool completely on a wire rack. Store at room temperature in a loosely covered container.

Note: If any sesame seeds are left over, put them in a plastic bag and store in a cool, dry place. They can be used for decorating any of the treats in this section.

Chapter 5

5th ave.

DECADENCE

For those with richer tastes

This collection of sweets strays from the path of the others by exploring combinations that are both indulgent and delightful. Some are simple, some are sinful. Like a stroll down Manhattan's 5th Avenue, where the riches of the world entice you, these goodies will have your dog pining by the cookie jar.

banana nut biscottys

2 ½ c. oat flour

2 ½ c. brown rice flour

2 tsp. baking powder

½ tsp baking soda

2 eggs

1 tsp. vanilla

1 Tb. honey

¼ c. finely chopped peanuts

½ c. bananas (mashed & pureed)

A small container of water

✳ ✳ ✳

Preheat oven to 325°. Mash bananas and puree in a food processor.

Combine all ingredients together in a food processor (or by hand in a bowl). Add 1 Tb. of water at a time until the dough reaches a workable consistency. Once the dough is formed, knead together by hand for several minutes on a lightly floured surface. Separate into two logs about 12" long by 4" wide and 1" high. Place on an ungreased cookie sheet.

Bake for 30 minutes. Remove and let cool on the baking sheet for 10 minutes. Slice pieces ½" thick. Bake an additional 20 minutes. Remove and place on a wire rack to cool completely. Store at room temperature in a loosely covered container.

cranberry scones

ε A perfect tea-time treat З

1 c. oat flour

1 c. brown rice flour

2 tsp. baking powder

1 c. dried cranberries

$\frac{1}{2}$ c. peanut butter (unsalted)

$\frac{1}{4}$ c. safflower oil

$\frac{1}{2}$ c. water

1 egg

✳ ✳ ✳

Preheat oven to 400°. Mix flours, baking powder, peanut butter, safflower oil, water (or chicken broth) and egg together in a food processor. Once combined, gently stir in cranberries by hand. Scoop out heaping spoonfuls onto an ungreased baking sheet (they do not spread, and barely rise, so they can be placed close together).

Bake 15-20 minutes or until a toothpick inserted into the center of the scone comes out cleanly. Remove from the oven and let cool completely. Store in an airtight container in the refrigerator.

☞ Berry, Berry Yummy

Several of the recipes in this chapter call for various berries, including cranberries, blueberries, and strawberries. Wonder no longer, all are safe for dogs. Berries are natural antioxidants; in fact, recent studies have shown that blueberries are especially rich in them. Cranberries are known for relieving urinary tract infections and promoting uterine health. Berries also contain lots of vitamin C. They are naturally sweet and tasty, and dogs really enjoy them. They can be served fresh, frozen, or dried.

mini
sweet potato pies

{ It's exactly what you think, only smaller }

FOR DOUGH:

1 c. oat flour

$^1/_2$ c. brown rice flour

$^1/_4$ c. safflower oil

$^1/_4$ c. water

1 egg

FOR FILLING:

1 c. cooked, mashed sweet potato

1 tsp. cinnamon

1 Tb. honey

1 tsp. ground cloves

1 egg

✳ ✳ ✳

Preheat oven to 400°. Cook and mash the sweet potatoes.

Combine all dough ingredients together and mix thoroughly. Roll out on a lightly floured surface to ¼" thickness. Divide evenly into 24 pieces and press them into the cups of a lightly greased mini muffin pan. Combine all the filling ingredients together and mix thoroughly. Scoop even amounts into each of the crusts in the muffin pan.

Bake for 15-20 minutes or until the edges of the crust are golden brown. Store in an airtight container in the refrigerator.

apple cinnamon muttins

   ξ *A tasty little treat that smells so good you'll want them for yourself* Ӟ

1 ½ c. oat flour

1 ½ c. brown rice flour

1 Tb. baking powder

1 tsp. cinnamon

2 eggs

³/₄ c. honey

1 c. applesauce (unsweetened)

¼ c. safflower oil

✳ ✳ ✳

Preheat oven to 350°. Combine all ingredients together and mix thoroughly. Place cupcake papers into a muffin pan. Spoon mixture evenly into the papers close to the top.

Bake 18-22 minutes or until a toothpick inserted into the center comes out clean. Remove from the oven and let cool completely on a wire rack. Store in an airtight container in the refrigerator.

the berry best oatmeal

{ A chewy treat that lives up to its name }

1 c. oat flour

1 c. rolled oats (old-fashioned kind, not instant)

$\frac{1}{4}$ tsp. baking soda

$\frac{2}{3}$ c. honey

$\frac{1}{4}$ c. safflower oil

2 $\frac{1}{2}$ c. blueberries (fresh or frozen)

✳ ✳ ✳

Preheat oven to 350°. Combine all ingredients (except blueberries) together and beat until evenly mixed. Separate the mixture in half. Lightly grease a muffin pan and press half of the mixture into the bottom of the muffin cups. Evenly spread the berries on top. Then sprinkle the remaining crumb mixture on top of the berries.

Bake for 30-35 minutes or until top is golden brown. Remove from the oven and let cool completely on a wire rack. Store in an airtight container in the refrigerator.

all dogs
go to heaven

*{ The perfect brownie –
loaded with carob & more carob on top }*

FOR BROWNIES:

2 c. oat flour

1 tsp. baking powder

5 Tbs. carob powder
   (can not be substituted with chocolate)

2 eggs

$^3/_4$ c. honey

$^1/_4$ c. safflower oil

$^1/_2$ c. non-fat vanilla yogurt (or use non-fat plain yogurt &
add 1 tsp. vanilla)

FOR FROSTING:

1 8-oz. package low-fat cream cheese (at room temperature)

4 Tbs. carob powder

Preheat oven to 350°. Combine all brownie ingredients together. Lightly grease a 9" square pan and pour mixture in.

Bake 30-35 minutes or until sides of brownies seem to be loosening from the pan. Cool completely in the pan.

In a separate bowl, mix together frosting ingredients. Spread frosting on top of cooled brownies. Slice into the individual sized portions. Store in an airtight container in the refrigerator.

Yogurt? You Bet!

Yogurt is another beneficial food that has been around forever. It is an excellent source of protein; because it has less milk sugar, it is easily digested, even by lactose-intolerant animals; it contains beneficial bacteria that support the digestive and immune systems; and it is a great source of calcium. A tablespoon or so of organic, plain, low-fat yogurt can benefit your dog in many ways; it is especially helpful when your dog is on antibiotics, as it restores some of the beneficial bacteria that the antibiotics randomly strip away or break down.

banana split personality

{ A banana that thinks it's a pumpkin }

1 ½ c. oat flour

1 ½ c. brown rice flour

1 c. rolled oats (old-fashioned kind, not instant)

1 tsp. cinnamon

2 eggs

¼ c. safflower oil

½ c. molasses (blackstrap or regular)

2 c. pumpkin (canned or fresh)

2 c. bananas (mashed & pureed)

❋ ❋ ❋

Preheat oven to 350°. Mash and puree the bananas.

Combine all ingredients together until thoroughly mixed. Lightly grease a 9" square baking pan. Pour mixture into it.

Bake 30-35 minutes or until top appears golden brown and sides begin to slightly loosen from the pan. Remove from the oven and let cool completely on a wire rack. Once cool, slice into individual-sized squares. Store in an airtight container in the refrigerator.

do I smell cake?

ε Watch out, it could ruin the surprise! з

FOR CAKE:

2 c. oat flour

½ c. carob powder (can not be substituted with chocolate)

1 tsp. baking powder

2 eggs

¼ c. safflower oil

½ c. honey

1 c. non-fat vanilla yogurt (or use non-fat plain yogurt & add

1 tsp. vanilla)

FOR ICING:

1 8-oz. package non-fat cream cheese (at room temperature)

1 Tb. honey

Preheat oven to 350°. Combine all ingredients together and mix thoroughly. Lightly grease a 6" round cake pan (preferably a 3" tall pan, but 2" is fine, too) and pour mixture into pan.

Bake 30-35 minutes or until a toothpick inserted in the center of the cake comes out clean. Remove from the oven and let cool completely on a wire rack.

In a separate bowl, combine icing ingredients. Once the cake is completely cooled, decorate with the icing. Store in an airtight container in the refrigerator.

if it ain't
a brownie...

{ *... then it's got to be a blondie!* }

2 c. oat flour

1 tsp. baking powder

2 eggs

$^1/_2$ c. honey

$^1/_4$ c. peanut butter (unsalted)

$^1/_4$ c. safflower oil

$^1/_2$ c. plain or vanilla non-fat yogurt

1 c. carob chips (can not be substituted with chocolate)

✳ ✳ ✳

Preheat oven to 350°. Combine flour, baking powder, eggs, honey peanut butter, oil and yogurt together in a large bowl. Stir in carob chips by hand until evenly mixed. Lightly grease a square 9" baking pan and pour mixture into the pan.

Bake 30-35 minutes or until the sides loosen from the pan and the top appears golden brown. Remove from the oven and let cool completely on a wire rack. Once cool, slice into individual-sized portions. Store in an airtight container in the refrigerator.

blueberry
muttins

E A favorite treat of humans,
and a favorite with dogs! 3

2 c. oat flour

2 tsp. baking powder

1 tsp. cinnamon

1 tsp. baking soda

2 c. blueberries (fresh or frozen)

3 eggs

¼ c. honey

¼ c. safflower oil

✳ ✳ ✳

Preheat oven to 350°. Combine all ingredients together and mix thoroughly. Place cupcake papers into a mini muffin pan (or a regular muffin pan). Spoon mixture evenly into the papers almost to the top (the mix will not rise very much).

Bake 10-15 minutes if using the mini muffin pan or 22-27 minutes if using a regular-sized muffin pan. Muffins are done when a toothpick inserted into the center comes out clean. Remove from the oven and let cool completely on a wire rack. Store in an airtight container in the refrigerator.

frozen yogurt smoothies

{ An icy treat to be enjoyed from sunrise to sunset }

FROZEN SUNRISE:

2 c. fruit juice (apple varieties work great)

1 mashed & pureed banana

1 c. plain non-fat yogurt

1 c. pureed strawberries

BLUE MOON:

2 c. non-fat plain yogurt

1 c. pureed blueberries (fresh or frozen)

2 Tb. honey

Combine all ingredients (from either variation) together and whisk thoroughly. Pour mixture into small cups (3" bathroom or kitchen paper cups work great). Freeze until solid (at least 4 hours).

Push the bottom of the cup to pop the treat out and serve to your pup.

ice cubes just got a lot better

❧ *A truly crunchy peanut butter treat* ❧

3 c. plain non-fat yogurt

1 c. peanut butter (unsalted)

1 Tb. honey

Combine all ingredients together and whisk thoroughly. Pour mixture into ice cube trays and freeze solid (at least 2 hours).

Pop out one cube at a time and serve to your pup.

teenie weenie banana barkinis

Keep that figure lean and mean!

FOR CUPCAKES:

2 c. oat flour

2 tsp. baking powder

$1/2$ tsp. baking soda

1 tsp. cinnamon

$1/2$ c. finely chopped walnuts

3 eggs

$1/4$ c. honey

3 bananas, mashed & pureed

$1/4$ c. safflower oil

FOR ICING (OPTIONAL):

1 c. banana, mashed & pureed

1 8-oz. package non-fat cream cheese (at room temperature)

1 tsp. vanilla

Preheat oven to 350°. Peel, mash and puree the bananas (for the cupcakes).

Combine all cupcake ingredients together in a large bowl. Place cupcake papers in a mini muffin pan and spoon the mixture into the cups evenly. Fill almost to the top of the papers as the cupcakes donít rise very much.

Bake 12-15 minutes or until a toothpick inserted in the center of a cupcake comes out clean. Remove from the oven and let cool completely on a wire rack.

Peel, mash and puree the remaining banana for the frosting. In a separate bowl, combine icing ingredients together and mix thoroughly. Decorate the mini cupcakes. Store in an airtight container in the refrigerator.

zucchini bread

Dogs enjoy their version of this treat as much as people do

2 c. oat flour

2 tsp. baking powder

½ tsp. baking soda

1 tsp. cinnamon

3 eggs

1 tsp. vanilla

¾ c. honey

2 c. pureed zucchini

¼ c. safflower oil

½ c. finely chopped walnuts (optional)

Preheat oven to 325°. Peel, slice and puree zucchini in a food processor.

Combine all ingredients together and mix thoroughly. Lightly grease a mini loaf pan (or use a regular muffin pan with cupcake papers placed in it). Spoon mixture evenly into the pan close to the top (the mix will not rise very much).

Bake 20-25 minutes (with either pan). Bread is done when a toothpick inserted into the center comes out clean. Remove from the oven and let cool completely on a wire rack. Store in an airtight container in the refrigerator.

☞ Zucchini's Zogood

Zucchini is one of several squashes that were a mainstay of Native American diets for centuries. These large, green vegetables are loaded with folate and potassium. Their rinds are rich in beta-carotene and should always be included in any recipe featuring this versatile squash.

peanut brittle

ƹ *It'll inspire you to break out the pinochle!* Ʒ

3 c. brown rice flour

1 tsp. cinnamon

1 egg

$^1/_2$ c. honey

$^1/_4$ c. molasses (blackstrap or regular)

$^1/_2$ c. peanut butter (unsalted)

$^1/_4$ c. safflower oil

1 c. finely chopped peanuts (unsalted)

Preheat oven to 325°. Combine flour, cinnamon, egg, honey, molasses, peanut butter and safflower oil in a food processor until completely mixed. It should form a stiff dough. Lightly grease a jelly roll pan and press the dough into the pan. Place plastic wrap or parchment paper over the pan and smooth down the mixture to $^1/_4$" thick. Remove and discard wrap or paper. Press the remaining chopped peanuts into the mixture. Use a knife to score the dough into individual sized portions.

Bake 30-40 minutes or until the edges are golden brown. Cool completely in the pan on a wire rack. Once cool, break apart using the scored lines. Store in a loosely covered container at room temperature.

pup tarts

❦ No toaster needed for these delicious snacks! ❧

FOR DOUGH:

1 c. oat flour

$\frac{1}{2}$ c. brown rice flour

1 egg

$\frac{1}{4}$ c. safflower oil

$\frac{1}{4}$ c. water

FOR FILLING:

$\frac{1}{2}$ c. blueberries (fresh or frozen)

$\frac{1}{2}$ c. diced strawberries (fresh or frozen)

1 tsp. vanilla

$\frac{1}{2}$ c. peanut butter (unsalted)

1 egg

Preheat oven to 400°. Combine all dough ingredients together and mix thoroughly. Roll out on a lightly floured surface to $\frac{1}{4}$" thickness. Divide evenly into 24 pieces and press them into the cups of a lightly greased mini muffin pan. Stir all the filling ingredients together and mix thoroughly. Scoop even amounts into each of the crusts in the muffin pan.

Bake for 15-20 minutes or until the edges of the crust are golden brown. Store in an airtight container in the refrigerator.

because I carob 'bout you

1 c. oat flour

1 c. brown rice flour

2 tsp. baking soda

$\frac{1}{2}$ tsp. baking powder

$\frac{1}{4}$ c. carob powder (can not be substituted with chocolate)

1 egg

2 Tb. honey

$\frac{1}{4}$ c. water

$\frac{1}{4}$ c. safflower oil

$\frac{1}{2}$ c. plain non-fat yogurt

✳ ✳ ✳

Preheat oven to 350°. Combine all ingredients together and mix thoroughly. Place cupcake papers into a mini muffin pan (or a regular muffin pan). Spoon mixture evenly into the papers close to the top of the papers (the mix will not rise very much).

Bake 10-15 minutes if using the mini muffin pan or 20-25 minutes if using a regular sized muffin pan. Cupcakes are done when a toothpick inserted into the center comes out clean. Remove from the oven and let cool completely on a wire rack. Store in an airtight container in the refrigerator.

Note: These can be iced with one of the icing recipes described in earlier recipes.

trail chasers

ξ Trail mix without the bag ʒ

2 c. oat flour

1 tsp. baking powder

$^{1}/_{2}$ c. peanut butter (unsalted)

$^{1}/_{2}$ c. rolled oats (old-fashioned kind, not instant)

$^{1}/_{2}$ c. finely chopped peanuts (unsalted)

$^{1}/_{2}$ c. shredded coconut (unsweetened)

$^{1}/_{2}$ c. dried cranberries

$^{1}/_{2}$ c. carob chips (can not be substituted with chocolate)

2 eggs

$^{1}/_{2}$ c. honey

1 tsp. vanilla

1 c. water

$^{1}/_{4}$ c. safflower oil

Preheat oven to 350°. Combine all ingredients together and mix thoroughly. Lightly grease a 9" square baking pan and pour mixture into it.

Bake for 30-35 minutes or until top is golden brown. Remove from the oven and let cool completely on a wire rack. Once cool, slice into individual-sized portions. Store in an airtight container in the refrigerator.

☞ A Taste of the Tropics

The Coconut Research Center in Colorado has this to say about the benefits of coconut: "Coconut is highly nutritious and rich in fiber, vitamins, and minerals. It is classified as a 'functional food' because it provides many health benefits beyond its nutritional content. Coconut oil is of special interest because it possesses healing properties far beyond that of any other dietary oil and is extensively used in traditional medicine among Asian and Pacific populations. Pacific Islanders consider coconut oil to be the cure for all illness. The coconut palm is so highly valued by them as both a source of food and medicine that it is called 'The Tree of Life.' Only recently has modern medical science unlocked the secrets to coconut's amazing healing powers." Use unsweetened coconut for dogs, but consider feeding it more often!

pumpkin muttins

*ℰ Dogs love the taste of pumpkin,
and it helps their digestive system, too ℥*

2 c. oat flour

2 tsp. baking powder

2 tsp. cinnamon

$1/2$ tsp. baking soda

$1/2$ tsp. ground cloves

3 eggs

$3/4$ c. honey

$1/4$ c. safflower oil

1 15-oz. can pumpkin (or fresh pureed pumpkin)

✳ ✳ ✳

Preheat oven to 350°. Combine all ingredients together and mix thoroughly. Place cupcake papers into a mini muffin pan (or a regular muffin pan). Spoon mixture evenly into the papers close to the top of the papers (the mix will not rise very much).

Bake 10-15 minutes if using the mini muffin pan or 22-27 minutes if using a regular sized muffin pan. Muffins are done when a toothpick inserted into the center comes out clean. Remove from the oven and let cool completely on a wire rack. Store in an airtight container in the refrigerator.

the
elvis pupsleys

{ Peanut butter and banana, baby! }

2 c. oat flour

1 tsp. baking powder

$1/2$ tsp. baking soda

$3/4$ c. carob chips

2 eggs

1 c. bananas (mashed & pureed)

1 c. peanut butter

1 tsp. vanilla

1 Tb. honey

$1/4$ c. safflower oil

✳ ✳ ✳

Preheat oven to 350°. Peel, mash and puree bananas in a food processor.

Combine all ingredients together and mix thoroughly. Place cupcake papers into a mini muffin pan. Spoon mixture evenly into the papers close to the top of the papers (the mix will not rise very much).

Bake 10-15 minutes or until a toothpick inserted into the center comes out clean. Remove from the oven and let cool completely on a wire rack. Store in an airtight container in the refrigerator.

Note: These can be iced with one of the icing recipes described earlier, but the King wouldn't have them any other way.

cheesecake
brownies

{ *Two great tastes that taste great together* }

2 c. oat flour

1 tsp. baking powder

5 Tbs. carob powder
  (can not be substituted with chocolate)

1 c. carob chips (can not be substituted with chocolate)

2 eggs

1 8-oz. package non-fat cream cheese

$^{1}/_{4}$ c. honey

1 tsp. vanilla

$^{1}/_{4}$ c. safflower oil

✳ ✳ ✳

Preheat oven to 325°. Combine all ingredients together and mix thoroughly. Lightly grease a 9" square baking pan and pour mixture into it.

Bake for 30-35 minutes or until sides loosen from the pan slightly. Remove from the oven and let cool completely on a wire rack. Once cool, slice into individual sized portions. Store in an airtight container in the refrigerator.

Note: These can be iced with one of the icing recipes described earlier.

because you have
UNIQUE
TASTES

Here are some specialties that meet your needs

Wouldn't it be nice if we could all eat exactly what we wanted any time we wanted it? If you don't think so, your dog certainly does (especially now that you're making all these great treats!). Our bodies, however, aren't built to take that kind of abuse – and neither are those of our dogs. Add to that individual problems like allergies, sensitive stomachs, and so on, and it can sometimes seem like finding anything to eat is a chore. This collection of treats is designed to soothe (the bodily irritations of) the savage beast, while providing flavor and variety. At last!

Note: Choose to use organic ingredients in these recipes, as we do when we make them.

under the harvest moon

{ A cornucopia of earthly delights }

1 c. oat flour

1 c. brown rice flour

$\frac{1}{2}$ c. rolled oats (old-fashioned kind, not instant)

$\frac{1}{2}$ c. hulled sunflower seeds (unsalted)

$\frac{1}{2}$ c. pureed carrots

$\frac{1}{2}$ c. cooked, pureed butternut squash

$\frac{1}{2}$ c. pureed broccoli

1 egg

$\frac{1}{4}$ c. water

These treats are high in fiber, low in fat,
meat-free, and low in protein.

Preheat oven to 350°. Peel, dice and finely grind carrots in a food processor. Cook, dice and finely grind butternut squash in a food processor. Finely grind broccoli in a food processor.

Combine all ingredients together in a food processor (or mix by hand in a bowl) until a dough forms. Spoon mixture out with a tablespoon and drop onto an ungreased cookie sheet. These cookies will not rise or flatten, so if you want a flatter cookie, press it down before baking.

Bake 20-25 minutes. Remove from the oven and let cool completely on a wire rack. Store in an airtight container in the refrigerator.

 # Carrots for Breakfast

And lunch, and dinner. Organic carrots are a wonderful regular addition to your dog's diet. They're naturally sweet, crunchy, and nutritious. Many feed their dogs mini carrot sticks as snacks – and dogs love them! Carrots are an exceptional source of vitamins A and C, as well as potassium. They are also high in fiber. Carrots supply nutrients necessary for the health of the eyes, immune and digestive systems.

pupeyes

ξ *All I needs is me spinachk* ʒ

1 c. oat flour

1 c. brown rice flour

$^1/_2$ c. grated parmesan cheese

1 c. tightly packed spinach leaves

1 egg

$^1/_2$ c. water

✳ ✳ ✳

This is a high-fiber, meat-free treat.

Preheat oven to 350°. Puree spinach leaves in a food processor until smooth.

Combine all ingredients together and mix until a dough forms. Roll into small balls (about 1" in diameter) and place on an ungreased cookie sheet (they can be rather close together as they don't spread while cooking).

Bake 20-25 minutes. Remove from the oven and let cool completely on a wire rack. Store in an airtight container in the refrigerator.

☞ The "Eyes" Have It

That's "pupeyes" for anyone who's confused. And they "have it," because these treats pack a one-two punch in terms of nutrition and taste. The ingredient combo in these treats is one of the best out there: whole grains, spinach, egg, and cheese. That's energy to burn, and energy to spare. And no shortage of flavor! You may find yourself snacking on these, too!

ohm my these are good

{ Helps their bellies achieve a zen-like state }

1 c. oat flour

1 c. brown rice flour

½ c. canned pumpkin (or fresh pureed pumpkin)

1 tsp. cinnamon

1 egg

⅓ c. water

These treats are high in fiber, low in fat,
meat-free and low in protein.

Preheat oven to 350°. Combine all ingredients together and mix until a dough forms. Roll into small balls (about 1" in diameter) and place on an ungreased cookie sheet (they can be rather close together as they don't spread while cooking).

Bake 20-25 minutes. Remove from the oven and let cool completely on a wire rack. Store in an airtight container in the refrigerator.

philly-style

1 ½ c. tapioca flour
  (or garbanzo bean flour, or amaranth flour)

1 8-oz. package low-fat cream cheese

2 6-oz. cans of wild salmon

This treat is grain-free.

Preheat oven to 350°. Empty entire cans of salmon (juices included) into a food processor and puree.

Combine all ingredients together and mix thoroughly. Line a 9" square pan with parchment paper (it makes clean up easier). Pour mixture into pan.

Bake 30-40 minutes. Remove from the oven and let cool completely on a wire rack. Slice with a pizza cutter or knife into individual sized portions. Store in an airtight container in the refrigerator.

I yam what I yam

{ I am a yam }

1 ½ c. oat flour

1 ½ c. brown rice flour

2 c. cooked, mashed yams (or sweet potatoes)

1 c. oat bran

1 Tb. honey

1 egg

⅓ c. water

*These treats are high in fiber, low in fat,
meat-free, and low in protein.*

Preheat oven to 350°. Cook and mash yams. Place in a food processor to make smooth.

Combine all ingredients together and mix until a dough forms. Roll out on a lightly floured surface to ¼" thickness. Use any shape cookie cutter or a knife to cut out shapes.

Place on an ungreased cookie sheet (they can be rather close together as they don't grow much while cooking).

Bake 20-25 minutes. Remove from the oven and let cool completely on a wire rack. Store in an airtight container in the refrigerator.

☞ Flying Treats

No, these won't jump out of the cookie jar and fly away, but you will find that your dog so loves them that you will fly through a batch. Like pumpkins, yams are full of potassium, fiber, beta-carotene, vitamins and minerals. Mixed with oats and honey, they turn into little "sweet potato pies" – irresistible!

herban renewal

1 c. oat flour

1 c. brown rice flour

$^1\!/_2$ c. oat bran

$^1\!/_2$ c. cottage cheese (the lower the fat, the better)

1 tsp. dried rosemary

1 tsp. dried parsley

1 tsp. dried oregano

1 tsp. dried sage

1 egg

$^1\!/_3$ c. water

This treat is low in fat, high in fiber, and meat-free.

Preheat oven to 350°. Combine all ingredients together and mix until a dough forms. Roll out on a lightly floured surface to ¼" thickness. Use any shape cookie cutter or a knife to cut out shapes. Place on an ungreased cookie sheet (they can be rather close together as they don't grow much while cooking).

Bake 20-25 minutes. Remove from the oven and let cool completely on a wire rack. Store in an airtight container in the refrigerator.

 Herbs for Life

Whole books have been written on herbs and their health benefits. Sidebars in other chapters of this book have detailed the benefits of some of those most commonly used in dog food (and specifically the treats in this book!). Two particularly interesting websites to visit to learn more include www.crystalgardenherbs.com and www.botanicalmedicine.org.

liver alone

ε *... but not in exile* ﻝ

1 ½ c. tapioca flour
   (or garbanzo bean flour or amaranth flour)

1 lb. beef livers (or chicken livers)

2 eggs

This treat is grain-free.

Because You Have Unique Tastes

Preheat oven to 300°. Puree liver in a food processor. Immediately clean it afterwards, as liver makes an awful mess if left in there to dry.

Combine all ingredients together and mix thoroughly. Line a jelly roll pan with parchment paper (it helps make clean up a breeze). Pour mixture into the pan.

Bake for 30 minutes. Cut into tiny individual sized portions using a pizza cutter or a knife. Remove from the oven and let cool completely on a wire rack. Store in an airtight container in the refrigerator.

Note: To make crunchier treats, put them back in the oven (after cutting them) for an additional 2 hours at 150°.

Grain-Free Flours

Even if your dog isn't gluten intolerant (and be thankful if he isn't), health experts advise going without wheat- and grain-based foods occasionally, and it's helpful to know what to substitute. This recipe is completely grain-free – and your dog won't notice, or care.

jerky turkey

*{ One tough bird, but one
gentle-on-the-tummy treat }*

1 lb. raw ground turkey (or chicken)

1 Tb. Extra-virgin olive oil

This treat is grain-free and low in fat.

Preheat oven to 200°. Combine all ingredients together in a food processor and puree the mixture. Line a jelly roll pan with parchment paper (it makes clean up easier) and pour the mixture into it. Spread evenly.

Bake 2 hours with the oven door slightly ajar to allow the moisture to escape. Remove from oven, and using a pizza cutter or knife, cut into small individual-sized portions. Place pieces back in the oven, flipped over, and bake an additional 1-2 hours or until the treats are dry and leathery. Store in an airtight container in the refrigerator.

☞ Gobbling Up Turkey

Turkey is a poultry that is becoming more and more available to consumers because it is naturally low in fat without the skin, containing only 1 gram of fat per ounce of flesh. It is also a good source of B vitamins, potassium, and zinc. Cooked with the skin on, the flavor is sealed in without adding additional fat.

cowboy snacks

❦ Keeps their hunger from stampeding ❦

1 lb. lean ground beef (or buffalo)

This is a grain-free treat.

Preheat oven to 200°. Puree the meat in a food processor. Line a jelly roll pan with parchment paper (it makes clean up easier) and pour the mixture into it. Spread evenly.

Bake 2 hours with the oven door slightly ajar to allow the moisture to escape. Remove from oven and using a pizza cutter or knife cut into small individual sized portions. Place pieces back in the oven, flipped over and bake an additional 1-2 hours or until the treats are dry and leathery. Store in an airtight container in the refrigerator.

Because You Have Unique Tastes

☞ Home on the Range

Long before settlers moved in and took over, Native Americans were thriving on the multiple blessings of the bison (commonly referred to as the buffalo). One of these was the quality of their meat. In short, bison contains more of what our bodies need – iron, protein, and fatty acids – and less of what we don't (fat, cholesterol, and calories). Because it is nutrient-dense, it can be consumed in lesser quantities than beef and still provide similar (if not increased) health benefits while contributing to a greater feeling of fullness. Your dog won't know this, but you will, and it is something to smile about.

tu–na fish is better than one

& And healthy, too, so have a few! 3

1 c. oat flour

1 c. brown rice flour

1 6-oz. can albacore tuna (in water)

$1/4$ c. oat bran

1 egg

$1/2$ c. water

* * *

This treat is low in fat.

Because You Have Unique Tastes

Preheat oven to 350˚. Empty all contents (including juices) from can of tuna into a food processor and puree.

Combine all ingredients together and mix until a dough forms. Roll out on a lightly floured surface to ¼" thickness. Use any shape cookie cutter or a knife to cut into individual sized portions. Line a cookie sheet with parchment paper (easier clean up). Place on cookie sheet (they can be rather close together as they don't grow much while cooking).

Bake 20-25 minutes. Remove from the oven and let cool completely on a wire rack. Store in an airtight container in the refrigerator.

going all the way...
upstream

{ Losing weight and winning the race, the salmon way }

1 c. oat flour

1 c. brown rice flour

1 6-oz. can wild salmon

$^{1}/_{4}$ c. oat bran

1 egg

$^{1}/_{2}$ c. water

✳ ✳ ✳

This treat is low in fat.

Preheat oven to 350°. Empty all contents (including juices) from can of salmon into a food processor and puree.

Combine all ingredients together and mix until a dough forms. Roll out on a lightly floured surface to ¼" thickness. Use a pizza cutter or a knife to cut into small bite-size pieces to be used for training. Line a cookie sheet with parchment paper (easier clean up). Place on cookie sheet (they can be rather close together as they don't grow much while cooking).

Bake 20-25 minutes. Remove from the oven and let cool completely on a wire rack. Store in an airtight container in the refrigerator.

 Salmon

This delicious, pink-fleshed fish is low in calories and saturated fat, high in protein, and rich in omega-3 fatty acids (the ones that are good for you). Wild-caught cold water fish, like salmon, are higher in omega-3 fatty acids than warm water fish. Salmon is also an excellent source of selenium, niacin and vitamin B12, and a good source of phosphorous, magnesium and vitamin B6.

cold turkey

❧ Your dog won't want to quit these delights ❧

1 c. oat flour

1 c. brown rice flour

1 c. raw ground turkey

1 tsp. dried rosemary

1 egg

½ c. water

This treat is low in fat.

Preheat oven to 350°. Combine all ingredients together and mix until a dough forms. Roll into small balls (about 1" in diameter) and place on an ungreased cookie sheet (they can be rather close together as they don't spread while cooking).

Bake 22-27 minutes or until cooked completely through. Remove from the oven and let cool completely on a wire rack. Store in an airtight container in the refrigerator.

dragon slayers

{ Helps to banish the foul beast that is bad breath! }

1 c. oat flour

1 c. brown rice flour

3 Tbs. applesauce (unsweetened)

$^1/_2$ c. dried mint

$^1/_2$ c. dried parsley

1 egg

$^1/_2$ c. water

This is a low-fat, meat-free treat.

Preheat oven to 350°. Combine all ingredients together and mix until a dough forms. Roll into small balls (about 1" in diameter) and place on an ungreased cookie sheet (they can be rather close together as they don't spread while cooking).

Bake 20-25 minutes. Remove from the oven and let cool completely on a wire rack. Store in an airtight container in the refrigerator.

resources

There are thousands of websites of interest to dog owners these days, and the number of books on natural care continues to grow, too (how fortunate for us and our dogs!). We've been to quite a few of the sites and read lots of books, and this is our list of recommendations.

ε Books on Nutrition Ʒ

Holistic Guide for a Healthy Dog, by Wendy Volhard and Kerry Brown (Howell Book House, 2000)

Dr. Pitcarin's New Complete Guide to Natural Health for Dogs and Cats, by Richard H. Pitcairn and Susan Hubble Pitcairn (Rodale, 200)

The Goldsteins' Wellness & Longevity Program: Natural Care for Dogs and Cats, by Robert S. Goldstein, VMD, and Susan Goldstein (TFH Publications, 2005)

ε Internet Reference Sites Ʒ

www.aspca.org
A wealth of information, including a list of substances that are poisonous to animals.

www.naturesvariety.com
Some very interesting articles about nutrition and the benefits of certain ingredients, as well as the benefits of raw food.

www.vet.cornell.edu/library/freeresources.htm
A reliable network of informative websites and articles on all aspects of animal care, nutrition, behavior, disease, and so on.

ʒ Great Online Retailers ʒ

www.aid4greys.com
Besides being a not-for-profit business (all money raised goes to help retired racing Greyhounds), they make the best large bunny chew toys. Dogs just love them!

www.onlynaturalpet.com
A site dedicated to all natural products for dogs and cats.

www.uglydolls.com
The cutest damn chew toys ever made!

ʒ Online Communities ʒ

www.urbanhound.com
A great city-based resource for events, services, products, pet legal information, message boards, and much more.

www.wigglypups.com
A fun blog based out of NYC with good reviews and articles.

www.petsmo.com
An online networking site that also has good product reviews, advice, tips - even dating, if you're interested.

index

& About Bubba Rose Biscuit Co. 3

My husband Eric and I founded the Bubba Rose Biscuit Company in 2006 out of our desire to give our dogs healthier treats and food. Since the company's founding, we have been baking biscuits and making dogs happy from coast to coast – and even overseas.

Let us introduce the test group: We have the humans, Jessica and Eric Talley (co-founders of the company and co-authors of this book) - animal lovers and rescuers since day one. The list of pets we've cared for, prior to the pups, includes: guinea pigs, gerbils, sugar gliders, bunnies, a turtle, chameleons, a collared lizard, geckos, tree frogs, water frogs, fish, a snake, and a cat. There's no shortage of animal love and experience here.

And we have the pups: Bob (also called Bubba, Bobby Sue, Meat, and Biscuit), our beloved rescued Pit Bull. He's the sweetest, most affectionate 60-pound lap dog ever. Then there's Rose (also called Miss Rosetta [her racing name], Goose, Mama, and Greyhound), our precious Greyhound. She is the most delicate, intelligent, and gentle dog - and lazy as can be! And gone but not forgotten, we have Weeble (or Little Man, Monster and Stinky), he was our wacky little rescued Shih Tzu puppy. He was the happiest and most playful little guy. He has passed on since the first printing, but he's always in our hearts.

That's the gang (at present). And we have to get back to baking now – there are some hungry dogs waiting on us!

Visit us at ☞ www.bubbarose.com